The Japanese Nobel Prize winner Kawabata Yasunari (1899-1972) described the poems of Gotō Miyoko as "a stream of lyrics along which one follows the life of a distinguished poet."

Edward Seidensticker, fine translator of significant Japanese works, including the 11th Century *Tale of Genji*, one of Gotō Miyoko's primary sources of pleasure and inspiration, adds "it is a pleasure and honor to be a small part of the book."

A traditional yet independent woman of powerful passion born just after Japan began its transformation into a modern industrial nation, Gotō Miyoko championed deep changes in women's education and status. She revitalized the 1200 year old tanka tradition to reflect through the lense of her own life the paradoxes faced by each Japanese and the nation as a whole.

*

The TANKA is the Japanese traditional "short song" from which emerged the still shorter HAIKU.

"Miyoko's poems are personal ... pure and intense, and their freshness is a wonder."

Kawabata Yasunari
Nobel Prize in Literature, 1968

Japanese names are given in the traditional order, family name first.

Asian Poetry in Translation: Japan

Editor, Thomas Fitzsimmons

Supported by the National Foundation for the Arts, the Japan-US Friendship Commission,
Oakland University (MI), University of Michigan Center for Japanese Studies, and UNESCO.

I Am Alive

The Tanka Poems of Gotō Miyoko, 1898-1978

Asian Poetry in Translation: Japan #10

Dedicated to
Professor Gotō Shigeru

I Am Alive

The Tanka Poems of Gotō Miyoko, 1898-1978

Translated
with Introduction, Commentary and Notes
by REIKO TSUKIMURA

Preface by EDWARD SEIDENSTICKER

KATYDID BOOKS
Oakland University   Michigan

This publication was made possible by funds from the Risshun Tanka Society in Japan.

The Japanese text and the romanized first line index were produced on the Xerox Star Multilingual Work Station 8000 Series donated to the University of Toronto by the Xerox Cooperation University Grant Program.

Produced by KT DID Productions
Editorial Assistant: Susan K. Nara
Typeset by Susan K. Nara
Printed in the United States of America by Thomson-Shore, Dexter, MI

This book is printed on acid-free paper and its binding materials have been chosen for strength and durability.

Library of Congress Cataloging in Publication Data

Gotō, Miyoko, 1898-1978.
　　I am alive.

　　(Asian poetry in translation. Japan ; #10)
　　1. Gotō, Miyoko, 1898-1978--Translations, English. 2. Waka--Translations into English. 3. Waka, English--Translations from Japanese. I. Tsukimura, Reiko, II. Seidensticker, Edward, 1921-　　III. Title. IV. Series.
PL828.08A28 1988　　895.6'15　　88-8378
ISBN 0-942668-18-9 (alk. paper)
ISBN 0-942668-19-7 (pbk. : alk. paper)

Cover art and book design by
Karen Hargreaves-Fitzsimmons

First Edition

10 9 8 7 6 5 4 3 2

Contents

Preface

Edward Seidensticker

Think of a syllabary of some fifty symbols which can be made to reproduce all the sounds in a language. When there is no limit upon the number that can be strung together there is no limit upon the things that can be said. Imagine, also, a rule that the syllables may be combined only in sets of thirty-one. Imagine further that a wide range of vocabulary and subject matter is ruled out, and that gibberish is too. I have no head for mathematics and cannot say what it would be, but the possible number of combinations is certainly finite.

We have here essentially the conditions laid down for a very conservative body of poetry, perhaps the most conservative in the literature of the world. The tanka, "short poem," also called the waka, "Japanese poem," has been composed in huge numbers for some twelve or thirteen centuries. Through perhaps half of them, perhaps a third, it was almost the only form people took the trouble to compose poems in at all. The total count of syllables was thirty-one selected from about fifty. They had to be arranged in five clusters each of which had to have a certain syntactic autonomy. Foreign words were for the most part excluded. So was gibberish. The subject matter was very largely limited to love and to nature, or the two combined, with amorous relationships treated obliquely through a repertory of natural images. One cannot but admire such sturdy fidelity and conservatism. Yet it is a wonder that they who were faithful to the tradition and all its conventions did not quickly run out of things to say.

The history of tanka does indeed contain great stretches of monotony. The patient delver into the courtly anthologies must surely wish from time to time, whatever his patience, that a few of the poems about cherry blossoms could instead be about dandelions, a few of those about maple leaves might rather be about poison oak.

Yet tanka poets went on finding variations. An even greater wonder is that from time to time there have been bursts of great vitality. It still proves possible to make thirty-one-syllable statements that not only avoid repetition but speak to us with power and urgency. Our own century has been such a time. Tanka poets have preserved the thirty-one-syllable form and in varying degree adhered to the conventional subject matter, and yet managed to speak with voices and to convey experiences and emotions that could only be of our time.

Mrs. Gotō was among the major poets in this modern renaissance. She sometimes chose themes and subjects that had not much been used before. Probably the most famous and popular of her poems are on motherhood, inspired chiefly by the tragic death of her older daughter. Sometimes she brought new life to old and much-used themes (overused, we might be tempted to say). For me the most remarkable of her poems are about cherry trees. She did not use the image, as so many earlier poets did, to signify evanescence or something of the sort. Rather she sought to convey the immediate experience of a cherry tree; and she succeeded. It is a remarkable achievement, among the notable ones of our time. A theme so old and worn that one might have thought it on the point of expiration is made to live once more.

I am unable to resist introducing a personal note. For me this book is like a gathering of friends. Here is Mrs. Gotō, a friend from my student days, not far from forty years ago. We and several other students of the late Professor Ikeda Kikan and the professor himself sat together in a cold dark room for several hours one afternoon each week and pushed our way through *The Tale of Genji*. It was the first time I had read the original text, and a memorable experience. (The room was not always cold, but somehow in memory it is.) Here is Professor Tsukimura, a friend of not quite such long standing, but of several decades even so. And here am I. It is a pleasure and an honor to be a small part of the book.

Introduction

Japan's Nobel Laureate Kawabata Yasunari (1899-1972) described the poetry of Gotō Miyoko (1898-1978) as "a stream of lyrics along which one follows the life of a distinguished poet." [1] As this description suggests Miyoko's poems can be read as an autobiography in the form of the traditional tanka short poem.

A long career marked by both success and tragedy culminated in such honors as being appointed tanka instructor to the Crown Princess of Japan, and being decorated with the Order of Purple Ribbon for her contributions to Japanese culture. Some of the poems translated here reflect this public aspect of the poet. Most interesting, however, are Miyoko's relationships with the members of her family. By turning her life into powerful and intimate poems she succeeded in achieving an inimitable style characterized by emotional intensity and rhythmic spontaneity.

Written over some sixty years Miyoko's tanka reflect in microcosm Japan's struggle for identity as a modern nation. Here is a mirror in which one catches sharp glimpses of a woman full of the fascinating paradoxes that could be found in almost any Japanese who underwent the transformation of the first three decades of the twentieth century. Miyoko was traditional and inhibited, yet at the same time progressive and liberated; though shy and cautious, she was a strongly independent woman of powerful passions.

Born just three decades after Japan launched its vigorous endeavor to modernize itself Miyoko retained an inherent sense of traditional values, a stability reflected in her conservative outlook -- as a teenage poet she memorized the tanka of Emperor Meiji (1852-1912) and Empress Dowager Shōken (1849-1914) and was enthralled by the canonical tenth-century imperial tanka collection, *Kokinshū*; [2] later she admired her royal student, the Crown Princess. She was also, however, deeply involved in the proletarian tanka movement in 1929-30.

Throughout, Miyoko's poetry gained depth and breadth, adding political and cosmopolitan dimensions.

Combining conservatism and modernism helped Miyoko rediscover and revitalize the tanka tradition, an achievement best exemplified in her tanka on *The Tale of Genji* and in her efforts to bring back through contacts with proletarian and amateur poets the vigor and freshness tanka once possessed before the long process of conventionalization. Having to work from a tradition at least twelve hundred years old Miyoko became a masterful practitioner who never hesitated to violate formal rigidity and abandon the narrowness of simple refinement in her effort to treat new topics demanded by her modern perception and international experiences. Even her most private poems share this expansiveness which illuminates a whole range of human relationships between four generations of women -- her mother, Miyoko herself, Miyoko's daughters and her only granddaughter -- all of them typically, but not only, Japanese. Miyoko's deeply involved and involving experiences of love, anger, hatred, anxiety and joy achieve an extraordinary intensity.

In 1956 Miyoko and six other women tanka poets interviewed Murō Saisei (1889-1962), novelist and poet, for their journal, "*Nyonin tanka*" ("Women's Tanka"; founded, 1949), [3] and discussed the difference between the two representative traditional Japanese poetic forms, tanka and haiku.

Formally, tanka (which comes, at the latest, from the seventh century) consists of thirty-one syllables in five units of 5,7,5,7,7. Haiku (derived from the first verse of *renga*, linked verses that flourished in the fifteenth century) corresponds to the first three units (5,7,5) of tanka.

Other differences were suggested by Saisei. A novelist who wrote haiku, but not tanka, he defined tanka as *shōsetsuteki* (novelistic), and haiku as *dōtokuteki* (moralistic). One woman observed that though much had changed in haiku, its emphasis is still the purity of a white chrysanthemum. "Tanka," Miyoko added, "looks for the dust."

What Saisei meant by the term "novelistic" is that tanka contains an element of narrative, and is populated by humans involved with emotional, mental, spiritual, or physical action. Such human involvement, however, is not the focus of haiku; there nature predominates and humans fade into the background, harmonizing with it.

Compare the following two poems. First, a haiku, by Japan's greatest haiku poet, Matsuo Bashō (1644-1694), that Saisei considered exceptional in that it focuses on women:

In the same inn
prostitutes also sleep
bush clover and the moon.

Prostitutes also appear in an early tanka of Miyoko:

Casting
envious glances
at my child
prostitutes roam the streets,
lipstick bright.
> (The Poems, #36)

While the haiku maintains a distance, the tanka involves itself. According to Saisei narrative and non-moral elements have been part of tanka throughout its 1200 year history.

Miyoko's poetry is also "novelistic" in its exploration of the poet's private life.

Three years before the interview with Saisei, Miyoko published, in 1953, *Haha no kashū* (*Tanka Poems of a Mother*), a selection from four previous books of poems mostly about her two daughters that appeared after Miyoko's recovery from the devastating loss of her beloved twenty-three-year-old daughter. This collection can be read as a mother's poetic autobiography following the daughters' development and the mother's emotions. Her children, in fact, became Miyoko's major topic, and she is sometimes known as *bosei kajin* (tanka poet as mother).

Not always, however, a gentle, affectionate mother. Miyoko herself has said about her tanka that they have an animal smell.[4] The power of her attachment to her children often carries her beyond what we call "common sense," sometimes even seems to border on madness. When the Sino-Japanese War broke out in July, 1937, shortly after her second daughter's birth, Miyoko, preoccupied with her children's safety, was shocked at the strength of her feelings.

Sometimes
I feel I have the heart of
Kishimojin,
the demon mother who butchered
other children to feed her own.
(The Poems, #56)

In 1953, before the burial of her older daughter's ashes, which she had kept at home for the unusually long period of three years, Miyoko wrote:

Almost choking
on her abundant youth,
breathlessly
my daughter lived -- I press
to my cheek one of her bones.
(The Poems, #147)

She compared her sorrow to that of the mother in a thirteenth-century Nō drama, *The River Sumida* in which the mother's grief for her lost son leads to insanity. [5]

Some critics, uneasy with Miyoko's openness about her private life, have called her poetry "ego-centric" and accused her of insensitivity to those she exposed to the public eye. Others, while recognizing the powerful integrity of her work, wish for a broader social and historical outlook. It seems to me, however, that Miyoko's poetry is able to transcend her private experiences precisely because it is so firmly grounded in them. Her integrity permitted her to go beyond petty conformity to social niceties, but she was sometimes disturbed that her poetry might possibly harm others. Still, she was unable to avoid becoming "the demon of tanka." [6]

When several friends encouraged her to write a novel Miyoko said "Should I ever write a novel, it would turn into a *shishōsetsu* (I-novel) [7] completely stripped of disguise. Moreover, I could not produce more than one in my whole life. I cannot understand anything that has not really happened, so ..." [8]

Miyoko rejected literary embellishment, and fiction for fiction's sake. Tanka, novelistic, non-moral and so brief as to leave little room for ornamentation provided her with a form into which she could pour her intensely personal experiences.

She was also apprehensive about too much intellectualizing in the poetic process:

> I do not disagree with the method of composing tanka by building parts into a structure. However, I sense a danger in a clever arrangement that may distort the order in which our impressions initially occurred. (HD, p. 239)

"Raw impressions" (*nama no kandō*) are central to Miyoko's poetics: she told her students to jot down impressions before they disappeared because they put us into three kinds of mental states from which poetry blossoms: "Being led to surprise; being led to a sigh; and being led to contemplation." [9] The purer these states, the lovelier the blossoms.

The "I-novelistic" (*shishōsetsuteki*) nature of her poetry finds strong favor with Tamaki Tōru (1924-), fine tanka poet and discerning critic: "Tanka should keep, with a stubborn determination, its I-novelistic approach." [10] The statement reflects his objection to a mistaken call for "ideas" which he fears would generalize specific personal experiences and reduce the literary act to mere conceptualization.

Specifics, not generalizations, fill Miyoko's poetry; pure and intense, they attain universal meaning. We do not have to know who she was thinking of in this poem:

Thunder roars,
cracks in my secret cleft;
there is
a person about whom I think
"Die."

       (The Poems, #163)

A critic has pointed out a possible allusion to Chapter 9, Book I of the *Kojiki* (*The Record of Ancient Matters* compiled in 712) [11] where Izanagi creates the islands of Japan through sexual union with Izanami. When Izanami dies giving birth to the fire-god, he kills this child and ventures into Hades to find her. There, despite her pleas not to do so, he enters the hall where she lays and finds her corpse -- "In her genitals was Crack-Thunder." Whether or not Miyoko's poem alludes to this scene, she expresses an archetypal anger all women can recognize.

The seeming simplicity of Miyoko's poetry, its narrow scope, straightforwardness, the naturalness of its flow all derive from an extraordinary emotional intensity, as best exemplified in this powerful, almost matter-of-fact comment on her older daughter's death:

On the day
she was born
my child lay
in this same position --
and just as silent.
　　　　　(The Poems, #131)

She also wrote out of some serene moments:

I woke
and found myself alive.
On my forehead
blossoms of mountain cherries
moist with morning dew.
　　　　　(The Poems, #142)

Miyoko adored cherry blossoms so much that people spoke of her *sakura kichigai* (cherry blossom craze).

　　　Miyoko also believed that the tradition of tanka flourished not through technical mastery but through the genuine expression of deeply-lived experiences. For twenty-two years, until two months before her death, she selected poems for the tanka column of the *Asahi Shinbun*, a major daily newspaper (**Poems 1950-59**) to which thousands of poems are submitted by persons of all ages and from all walks of life.

　　　In the latter half of the 1920s Miyoko broke away from the traditional language of tanka and wrote completely in the vernacular. Later she decided that these attempts, though earnest and sincere, did not result in "truly good tanka." What, then, is "truly good tanka"? As Miyoko wrote in *Watakushi no tanka* (*My Tanka*; 1957):

> Tanka is in fact a luminescent entity that emits an electric current. Indeed, only those tanka which attain this condition can be called truly good tanka. Words are nothing but a medium through which the current flows. The key to both the creation and appreciation of tanka lies in our discovery of words and rhythm which serve as good conductors. [12]

In her search for good conductors Miyoko was both traditionalist and unconventional. Though most of her tanka is written in classical Japanese, she frequently combined that with the vernacular to create a unique style that is free from the harshness and bluntness of everyday language while retaining its freshness. Finding in them a hope for good contemporary tanka, she showed great interest in colloquial tanka by teenage poets. [13]

Her view of rhythm was also both conservative and progressive. On the one hand she contended that abandoning the traditional syllabic rhythm would turn tanka into a short poem in no way distinguishable from modern free verse and objected to irregularities in syllabic count that could claim no necessity nor inevitability. On the other hand Miyoko is one of the celebrated tanka poets who have produced highly successful tanka that violate fixed rhythm. Though their surface rhythm does not strictly follow conventional syllabic pattern these tanka have a compelling inner rhythm that flows into the reader. This deeper rhythm, though it varies from poet to poet and from poem to poem, resonates with an intrinsic unity that distinguishes tanka from other forms. Tamaki Tōru, who analyzed the rhythm by examining tanka structure, explains its characteristics:

> Tanka is a lyric of thirty-one syllables in five units. But this syllable structure must be felt as one sentence. Actually, there are two sentences in some tanka, yet the two must be felt as one. [14]

Tamaki goes on to point out that a fundamental difference between haiku and tanka is that the unity of haiku is not based on this *perception as one sentence.*

To simulate in English the experience of Japanese tanka the translations in this book were made in accord with three principles:

> Not to reproduce the exact Japanese syllabic pattern, but to render a similar rhythmic flow by using the line pattern short-long-short-long-long;
>
> To avoid inversions, though these often are an easy solution for translating Japanese syntax into English;
>
> To avoid archaic words: tanka poets still prefer a classical Japanese that has developed, through a long process of refinement, words both brief and suggestive but often no longer used in spoken language. Modern English can convey these qualities of the classical Japanese.

Since Miyoko maintained that tanka is not just a short poem with no fixed form, so tanka in English must have form. The difference between the two languages, however, must be considered. Japanese has no consonantal clusters: syllables always consist of one vowel or of one consonant followed by a vowel. The possibility for rhyming is endless; to avoid that monotony, rhyme has never been developed in Japanese poetry. Syllabic pattern is the sole device that defines the tanka form.

It is sometimes argued that tanka must be written and translated into only one line, but this view slights the importance of the five syllabic units. Tanka rhythm based on this structure has been, to use Miyoko's words, "remembered for centuries by the blood" that runs in the Japanese people (HD, p. 244). Whether tanka is written in one line or more this structure is understood by the Japanese reader. Lacking this shared understanding, English tanka requires a form that does not exactly follow but simulates the original structure. The simulated form can best be achieved through line divisions.

The inner rhythm of Japanese tanka is conveyed through both the flow of the five syllabic units and the diverse effects produced by the tensions and links between the units. The translations here attempt to re-create in a five-line structure the interrelations of the original syllabic units. In principle this method respects Miyoko's view that she "would accept a relation to the fixed rhythm which is neither too close nor too remote." [15]

In his article "Form in Haiku," Eric Amann suggests:

Use three lines of which the first and the last should be symmetrical and about equal *in sound duration* (not in syllables). The second line should be a little longer in sound duration than the first and the last. (Italics Amann's)[16]

Attention to "sound duration" is important because long and double vowels are counted as two syllables in both haiku and tanka in Japanese.

Amann gives his second suggestion about haiku:

Observe line unity: Each line should be a self-contained unit. (Note how in Bashō's poem each line carries a single, separate image). [17]

This view takes us back to Tamaki's remark that the tanka structure is perceived as one sentence, even when there are actually two, and that this structure presents a clear distinction between tanka and haiku.

Reading Miyoko's poems aloud often reveals the line relationships (connections, breaks, and flow) that help conduct the electric flow of these poems. That current guided the translator; hopefully, it will flow out to the reader as well.

Acknowledgements

My initial interest in tanka goes back to my high school years in Japan. Some years later, in 1968, through Professor Uemura Etsuko of Japan Women's University, my Alma Mater, I was fortunate enough to meet Gotō Miyoko, already a well-known tanka poet. From then until the end of her life I corresponded with her, sending her my own attempts at tanka, some of which she was kind enough to include in her magazine, *Risshun*.

During this time I gradually realized the importance of introducing to the Western world this woman who created *tanka* from experiences that spanned the first three quarters of the century, a period in Japanese history that saw unprecedented changes in society and literature.

The *tanka* included in this volume were translated over many years. For the bulk of the book, including the final revisions and background material on Miyoko's life and poetry, I am indebted to people too numerous to mention.

I owe special thanks to the following scholars in North America: Professor Earl Miner of Princeton University; Professor Makaoto Ueda of Stanford and Professor Kenneth Yasuda of Indiana for their encouragement and valuable suggestions; Professor James Araki of Hawaii, who knew both the poet and her husband, for his enthusiastic response to my work and for his perceptive remarks; and last but not least, Professor Edward Seidensticker, distinguished translator of *The Tale of Genji*, who knew the poet well from the period immediately after World War II, not only for his invaluable comments throughout this endeavour but also for the privilege of his foreword to my book.

My study also benefited from critical works as well as the co-operation of the tanka poets Tamaki Tōru and Kondō Yoshimi, of the novelist Serizawa Kōjirō, and of the poet Ōoka Makoto. I should like to extend to each my heartfelt thanks.

I am grateful for grants from the Japan Foundation; the University of Toronto-York University Joint Center on Modern East Asia; the Social Sciences Humanities Research Council of Canada; and the

Department of East Asian Studies, University of Toronto. These grants enabled me to carry out my research both in Japan and Canada.

I gratefully acknowledge permission to reprint in revised translations poetry first published in *The Malahat Review, Contemporary Verse II, Arc* and *Risshun.*

I owe two special debts for editorial help: Dr. Eric Amann, Canadian poet and editor, who carefully read the manuscript and gave me many useful criticisms and suggestions, and Professor Thomas Fitzsimmons, poet/editor of the Asian Poetry in Translation Series, whose expert suggestions were incorporated in the final draft.

My thanks also are due to the Risshun Tanka Society, founded exactly fifty years ago by the poet and her husband. Besides providing me with assistance and encouragement the society honored my work with the Gotō Miyoko Literary Prize for 1983. I owe particular gratitude to Miss Sawa Yoshie, a founding member of the society, who began tanka writing in 1935 under the guidance of Mr. Gotō. I appreciate her inexhaustible kindness in answering my numerous questions and introducing me to the places in Osaka where the young Gotōs lived.

Finally, with deep gratitude I dedicate this book to Mr. Gotō Shigeru, who's devotion to collecting and editing his wife's poems greatly helped make them available to the Western reader.

The Poems
In English

POEMS 1924-30

Leaving
you behind, again I cross
the great river,
Tone. Water oats spread
along the bank, yellowing. [18]

2 [*] - 1924

Alone,
unable to sleep, I feel
my hair,
this dear black hair
that your breath touched.

3 - 1925

At the summer house in Karuno Village of Kashima. [19]

Heaven
and earth are suffused
with moonlight.
A sudden sense of wonder
at you and I together.

4 - 1925

---

[*] For poem #1 see 1898-1923: Commentary.

MOVEMENT IN THE WOMB (Poems 5-6)

Step by step
a life solemnly
forms in me.
Am I really
to be a mother at last?

5 - 1925

The baby
must be at peace
this morning
how quietly and gently
it moves in my womb.

6 - 1925

On April 22, 1926, Hitomi was born.

"Now we're parents"
we say to ourselves
silently,
looking at each other
in the diffused light of dawn.

7 - 1926

Tears
fall on my cheeks,
as I gaze
intently at my baby
now placed so close to me. [20]

8 - 1926

I mirror
my child's smile,
feeling strange
as though I were looking
at my own face.

9 - 1926

Whatever she picks up
seems dangerous to me
I snatch it
from my child's hands:
regret pierces me.

10 - 1926

Confronted
by something she longs
to say,
yet without words, the child
peers into my eyes.

11 - 1927

Scolded
mercilessly, the child
stands tight in fear;
her eyes at once
reflect her mother's.

12 - 1928

My daughter
shows me her drawing, "This is
Hanare Hill"
I see many roads
shooting up into the sky. [21]

13 - 1928

How can she
see those roads jutting
into the sky?
With my child in my arms I look
up at the hill, transformed.

14 - 1928

Her arms
stretched to the limit my child
reaches
for a caress; flower
turning to the sun

15 - 1928

IN ONE STAGE OF MY LIFE (1929-30)

Stubborn silence was my only resistance,
before.

16

My heart is worn out by struggles dark as a garbage can.
These plum blossoms are much too white.

17

How miserable I look in the fresh sun filled air!
I've come out of my room of books.

18

During lunch break a factory worker wanders into the field,
he whistles, lets the sky suck up his fatigue.

19

I watch my child at play.
Staring at me a laborer returns to his afternoon work.

20

The salty pickling paste is biting cold this morning.
Today again the sick and homeless will die in the streets. [22]

21

How flabby I am today:
just one chapped finger made me shake.

22

A despicable woman -- that's what I am still -- who thinks
the earth stops moving until her husband comes home.

23

I'm shoved around by housewives
frantically pawing a mound of bargains.

24

Nightwork abolished, we meet to celebrate.
I sit next to a little factory girl with deep shoulder tucks
    in her kimono. [23]

25

I listen to them quietly; long to plunge
like a bullet into their hard heads.

26

Their conclusions disappear with the cigarette smoke.
Waiters clean up the butts.

27

Assuming that my child won't have to do them,
do I pass unconcerned those at dangerous jobs?

28

A haggard mother runs to the factory,
her child racing after her; no time to wipe his nose.

29

At last the baby sucks firmly, but the afternoon work -
siren snatches away the breast.

30

Children clinging left and right the mother washes rice.
The western sun shines on her breasts.

31

Do not leave these women behind.
Their steps are slow because they carry those who
   will build tomorrow's world.

32

Silent children without lunch, do you sense each other's hunger,
patiently enduring your empty stomachs?

33

I fear the strength of these children who
gradually adjust to endless hunger.

34

A harsh chill as dawn approaches.
Until morning light revives you, children, don't catch cold.

35

POEMS 1931-39

WINTER IN PICCADILLY (Poems 36-38)

Casting
envious glances
at my child,
prostitutes roam thc streets,
lipstick bright.

36 - 1932

Suddenly
the lost look of mothers
appears
through rouge and powder:
faces of the street women.

37 - 1932

The day
quickly darkens --
still playing
on the pavement,
shabby children.

38 - 1932

In January 1933 I saw my husband off to Berlin and lived with my child in a flat in West Kensington. (Poems 39-41)

Suffused
with light, roofs glisten
white on white
this frosty morning.
Who first said we should live apart?

39 - 1933

Our lives
separate, days run off
one by one,
like the beads of a necklace,
snapped off and thrown away.

40 - 1933

Fretful,
like my suffering,
restless heart,
the reddish moon hangs
in the foggy sky.

41 - 1933

MONSOON
On the Indian Ocean on our way back to Japan.

"The monsoon is coming,"
someone calls from the bridge;
I am afraid, yet secretly thrilled.
My child is with me on this trip
so I tidy up my things
and go to bed, sleepless
nothing happens and the night ends.
Happy to see the dawn,
I climb to the deck and look out.
Relentlessly the engine echoes
the human will;
the masts stride along the sky road
waves break against the bow,
a path, foamy and white, opens behind the stern.
In this universe, sky above,
earth below, that's how I used to think;
on land that's what I believed.
Now this old thought retreats,
before the great Cosmos
I keep silent.
No end above, no end below,
no end before, behind, left or right;
the Indian Ocean, boundless,
stormy, is for a moment quiet.
Then I contemplate
my flesh and blood life:
If it is to end,

let death come now;
even dead, I'll be on this globe I love.
Such thoughts bring serenity.
Time passes slowly,
wind flutters the canvas.
Driving forward, the ship pitches heavily.
While I watch the horizon leaps high
into the sky, turns and slants,
sinks yards below the gunwale.
The storm comes, rushes me down to the cabin;
I shut the windows tight,
lean against the bed, breathless.
Through the small round windows
midday shines:
I keep still. Suddenly,
heavy and earth darken
I feel the boat
sink into the deep,
luminous waves crest
flow in torrents past the windows.
Then the turmoil is over, brightness everywhere,
but once again the ocean rises and
about to be swallowed, our ship pitches down.
My husband, a strong man,
unable to balance, falls.
My child, shaken comes to me,
I hold her to my breast,
murmur comforting words,
helpless as the lofty, overwhelming waves
shroud our space in utter blackness,

all but crushing the glass portholes
as I, mother of this child, barely hold on.

42 - 1933

Two envoys:

The windows
covered with surging foam --
my life floats,
surrounded by sea waves,
heaven and earth wrapped in mist.

43 - 1933

The sea
roars and undulates.
Drawn together,
father mother and child,
our lives become one life.

44 - 1933

HAVING LOST MY FATHER (Poems 45-47)

"I would like
to keep touching someone"
my father
says on his death bed
his mind still clear.

45 - 1935

How red
the pomegranate flowers
in the hospital garden
this brilliant summer;
my father didn't live to see them

46 - 1935

Two crickets
male and female, kept
by my father,
live on in their pot;
he is dead.

47 - 1935

MY YOUNG GIRL AND THE BABY IN MY WOMB (Poems 48-51)

Her eyes
moisten and shine;
my girl
so vulnerable lately,
a young woman peering out.

48 - 1936

A kicking in my body,
my heart content,
I abandon
myself to stirrings in my womb
throughout the night.

49 - 1936

Quietly
she snuggles up to me --
my daughter
is speaking, I am sure,
to the child in my womb.

50 - 1936

I breathe in
deeply the overflowing
rays of spring,
say to my unborn child,
"You also bathe in light."

51 - 1937

Stalks
of primroses grown tall
touch my body
in the last months of pregnancy.
How lovely they are.

52 - 1937

On May 8, 1937, the second daughter, Izumi, was born.

Still vivid
in my eyes,
the baby features
of my older daughter
overlap this newborn's face.

53 - 1937

Having decided to found the **Risshun** *in May 1938:*

The sky was
blue beyond the pines
that day, too,
when I, ardent and anxious,
picked this course of life. [24]

54 - 1938

I hug my child
my heart restless and fettered
by attachment;
not far from me, the worlds
of 'hungry spirits' and *ashura.*[25]

55 - 1938

Sometimes
I feel I have the heart of
Kishimojin,
the demon mother who butchered
other children to feed her own. [26]

56 - 1938

The cloudy mirror
has been left undusted --
my heart
long has lost its keenness.
I'm feverish again today.[27]

57 - 1938

For a while my hearing was weakened by influenza.

With ears now clear
this morning -- fondly I listen
to the voices
of my two children,
each with a tone of her own.

58 - 1938

Reading
my girlhood diary,
she chuckles:
my daughter is growing up
with a toughness I lacked. [28]

59 - 1939

Mother
and daughter, our souls will
separate some day.
Do I begin to see that moment
silently approaching?

60 - 1939

"What's in her heart?"
I watch her back,
hiding worries.
My daughter turns around,
gives me a happy look.

61 - 1939

My child,
two years old, walks
holding just
my little finger;
I feel her springy weight.

62 - 1939

On the ground
the shadow of my child
darkens;
I trace the shape of her ears,
and feel my love.

63 - 1939

Impossible
to avoid that feminine rite
of passage,
her eyes shining, at times yielding,
my daughter buds into a woman.

64 - 1939

Something
has happened in her body;
my thought
turns to it. My daughter
begins to blossom.

65 - 1939

POEMS 1940-47

Flames
blazing in my body,
I halt
where the wild waves of tide
climb and crash against this cliff.

66 - 1940

I spend a whole day among the cherry blossoms on Nara Hill.

At noontime
cherry blossoms overflow
in glory;
a black bird enters my mind,
darkening this spring day. [29]

67 - 1941

A golden bee
rests on a branch
at high noon,
sound muffled in the blossoms
of mountain cherries.

68 - 1941

Brief
as the tinkling of beads,
the sunlight
shifts: the flowers now are
absorbed into purple hues.

69 - 1941

Do the blossoms
mirror
my troubled mind,
take on paler hues? I wonder and
look, over and over again.

70 - 1941

Mother is seriously ill.

Marvelous!
she has won the battle
for life.
I stroke my mother
now tiny as a child.

71 - 1942

Mother dies on March 28, 1943. (Poems 72-73)

No longer
able to cover her body,
mother
lies under the light,
trusting her corpse to us. [30]

72 - 1943

Almost lost
in the shrouded sky
cherries
bloom in this land where
my mother no longer breathes.

73 - 1943

After August 15, 1945.

Humiliation
first experienced,
cold, bitter,
yet refreshing,
permeates my body. [31]

74 - 1945

Our nation
defeated, yet the mountains
and rivers
remain. I meet this spring
of brilliant flowers. [32]

75 - 1946

Blossoms
fall in dim light
I stand
hand in hand with my children,
feeling our warm blood.

76 - 1946

On the 1946 election in which women participated for the first time.

A silent word
from each of these women
as they quietly
leave the polling box,
their long submission now ended.

77 - 1946

No staple food for a long time.

A group of
little girls pick herbs
and many
younger boys catch crawfish
in the bright blue air.

78 - 1946

Endlessly
a dusty road stretches
in the ruins
of air-raid fires.
The sun burns in the noon sky.

79 - 1946

PREFATORY SONG TO *FIRE AND SNOW* [33]

As soon as I get up I have to shake my head:
my neck is sore again today and
my skin, like pine bark, dry
and sallow from shoulder to elbow.
In the past we would gladly
have died for our country, but
those days, illumined now by
one truth after another,
chill my heart, burn my face. [34]
Deeply tired in the morning I find
in the mirror a failing body
and stare into my eyes, my heart on fire.
Before this fire in me dies,

I, a woman, will rise once more
to consecrate my life to female songs
born of this time, new in our
two thousand years of history
proudly I will explore and sing.
So excited I gasp for breath
as my twenty year old daughter
peers from behind her lustrous hair.
Already a young woman she feels free,
speaks about all things human:
I see the path of this nation's women
shining far into the future
our children will achieve.
This cannot be a dream.

80 - 1946

Two envoys:

Yellow leaves
suffused by the sun
brighten the window
where mother and daughter
look into each other's eyes.

81 - 1946

For her and for me
infinite roads now open
to the blue sky --
I've abandoned the sweetness
of living for my children.

82 - 1946

Below
the rock hard ice lives
the fish --
I watch, sensing its eyes
pure and blue.

83 - 1946

My inner struggle
produces only a dry sound.
Helpless,
The short bamboo grass and I
are blown by the wind.

84 - 1946

Pushed
into the jammed train,
we all endure
in silence and peace,
swaying together.

85 - 1946

The loveliness
of blossoms fills the eye.
A petal
falls into the mud,
instantly, smeared.

86 - 1946

Though it warms to
The Tale of Genji and
the *Man'yō* poems,
my heart is still not content,
where does it go?[35]

87 - 1946

Over the filth
and confusion after the war
cherry blossoms
hover, radiant
in the luminescence of spring.

88 - 1947

No clouds
in the evening sky,
pale blue
lingers as if night
has forgotten to fall.

89 - 1947

Sharply,
unexpectedly, that grass smell
returns to me:
the fragrance of stems
nibbled in my childhood.

90 - 1947

Sweeping
midnight winds engulf
the moon
and me together.
Deep cold pervades.

91 - 1947

My hair flung back
I look up at the sky,
scornful
of slogans filling the streets:
"fall, muddy yourself." [36]

92 - 1947

Flushed
at noon, sizzling inside,
my body is cooled
by the late autumn wind
over the Musashi Plain. [37]

93 - 1947

My daughter
stands enveloped in light.
Sensing danger
I watch: the autumn wind
will snatch her away.

94 - 1947

Feeling
the blood warmth of our bodies,
are we shy
with each other, mother and child?
My daughter, too, averts her eyes.

95 - 1947

POEMS 1948-49

Frantic
for learning, I tear
myself
away from my child,
leave home again today.

96 - 1948

Waking
at midnight I think of
my father's brain
bottled in alcohol
at the Medical School. [38]

97 - 1948

I like to believe
something will pass on
to my children
when I have withered away
after this full life.

98 - 1948

To my daughter
I say, "Don't worry.
Follow
your own way." Yet I fear
what lurks in me.

99 - 1948

My eyes wide-open
I live in a corner
watching
spotlights slowly shift
as the world changes.

100 - 1948

My solitary body,
a withered branch
easy to ignite,
is blown about by the wind.
How long will this winter last?

101 - 1948

Late at night
my daughter and I dressed
our mother
no longer alive. Her body
still weighs in my hands.

102 - 1948

Nipples
red as flowers,
on the body
of my dead mother;
was it a vision only?

103 - 1948

Till the day
my mother was cremated,
faintly
a tint of red on her nipples
that none but I had sucked.

104 - 1948

In the falling
and melting snow
fire continues
to burn in me, now blazing,
now smoldering.

105 - 1948

When a poem
is born, life seems
whittled away;
I know such moments
and secretly fear them.

106 - 1948

I stand
in the chilly wind, my heart
recalling
an early rose in summer;
even its thorns were soft.

107 - 1948

Young grass
grows in a dusty,
withered field;
the smell of my child's hair
dirty so soon.

108 - 1948

I gaze at
the tiny trampled grasses;
my heart
softening, somehow I feel
redeemed.

109 - 1948

The waves
of a skipping rope billow
before me,
hesitant as a small child,
and always timid since.

110 - 1948

Softening
icicles sparkle,
drip,
trickle in the sun:
the valley is alive.

111 - 1948

The blood
of primeval ancestors
runs in me:
my whole heart thaws
when the earth warms.

112 - 1948

I think of
the bright other half
of this globe
as I lie in the darkness
of a spring night.

113 - 1948

IZUMI - YOUNGER DAUGHTER, IN AUTUMN (Poems 114-117)

My child,
still a little girl,
hesitant,
ready for womanhood,
changes from yesterday to today.

114 - 1949

Though I can't
be with you always,
bear it
and play, my child.
Your mother also has to grow.

115 - 1949

Did she notice
when she was left alone?
Bashfully
she talks about the beauty
of her body's curves.

116 - 1949

Like lovers
we accuse each other;
at last
we sleep quietly, holding
hands, mother and child.

117 - 1949

Hitomi, the apple of my eye [39]

My daughter
culls her words.
When she speaks,
they turn into little imps
and leap all about.

118 - 1949

When we see
we are hurting each other,
my daughter
and I, we both look up
to the *gingko* treetops.

119 - 1949

My daughter is restless,
the signs are clear:
she's ready
to take flight; how can I
hold her back in my stiff arms?

120 - 1949

REFLECTING ON *THE TALE OF GENJI* (Poems 121-130)

The Chinese white
is badly peeled, as I lean
over the scrolls,
the power of the black lines
hits my eyes. [40]

121 - 1949

Muffled
by the flowing mist,
music
floated on the river;
a dream of yesterday. [41]

122 - 1949

Silver paint
tarnished, the moon has
waned
over the centuries. Unaffected,
the words live on.

123 - 1949

The delicate feelings
of their hearts spill
from the five robes,
one over the other,
colors subtly fusing.

124 - 1949

Holding
much she wished to say
deep inside,
suspending breath,
she made a tale of wonder.

125 - 1949

From chapter
to chapter flowers and
emotions
come and go in crimson
edged with black.

126 - 1949

As she writes,
the stream of time runs
deep gray,
flowers scattering,
crimson leaves floating.

127 - 1949

Her gaze, sharp
and clear, penetrated
the screen
that hid the rich colors of nobles
moving in the smoke of incense.

128 - 1949

Modest and graceful,
yet so sharp, the eyes
of a woman
powerfully penetrated the world
outside the bamboo screens. [42]

129 - 1949

Light fades
as he vanishes --
purple sorrow
lingers until absorbed
into the void. [43]

130 - 1949

On January 26, 1950, Hitomi suddenly dies.

On the day
she was born
my child lay
in this same position --
and just as silent.

131 - 1950

In my arms
I hug my silent daughter.
abruptly
I hear time flying back
into the distant past.

132 - 1950

Don't soften
the sting of remorse
within me.
I will keep on living
as your very soul, your ghost.

133 - 1950

I watch
the pines sway in the wind,
enthralled
by this thought: my daughter
is surely alive among them.

134 - 1950

This body
which my full womb
once nourished,
what remains of it
among these ashes?

135 - 1950

The petals
of white lilies
turn pale blue
in the fading light:
still some ashes left unsifted? [44]

136 - 1950

Casually
one day my daughter said,
"Isn't Hitomi a good girl?"
What kept me from replying,
"Of course you are"?

137 - 1950

"I can live,"
I said to my daughter,
then still alive,
"just because the sky
is so beautiful."

138 - 1950

Did I lose you
for not saying
on that day,
"It's because of you
the sky is beautiful."?

139 - 1950

Its bridges set up
the *koto* is left
for the wind to stir,
like music, sounding
over the desolate winter hill. [45]

140 - 1950

In a dream
I, the only survivor
seek water,
moving among
my dead countrymen.

141 - 1951

I woke
and found myself alive.
On my forehead
blossoms of mountain cherries
moist with morning dew.

142 - 1951

Ceaselessly
wind blows over the chair
where my daughter
always sat, vacant now,
never to be used again.

143 - 1952

In her dream
my friend married
her dead son.
Did he enter once more
his mother's womb?[46]

144 - 1952

My lost child
fills Heaven and Earth.
The spring snow,
relentlessly falling,
soaks into my wound.

145 - 1952

I sense
in the pale moonlit garden
my lost child --
she pushes the swing,
her sleeves flying.

146 - 1953

Her ashes are buried on her birthday, April 22, 1953. [47]

Almost choking on
her abundant youth,
breathlessly
my daughter lived -- I press
to my check one of her bones.

147 - 1953

Hearts of hatred
explode in the sky,
ashes fall;
even mountain water
is not safe this summer. [48]

148 - 1953

In December 1953 Izumi is baptized a Catholic. [49]

My daughter
kneels to receive the blessings.
I stand
behind her facing the image
of the Holy Mother.

149 - 1953

My husband and
child have long been in bed.
Why am I excited
under the midnight lamp?
I push the window open.

150 - 1953

This poem was read at the January 12, 1954 New Year Poetry Party at the Imperial Court. [50]

Young branches
of *kunugi* bend, touch
my body
along a narrow path
on the woody hill. [51]

151 - 1954

I comb
my daughter's long hair.
Suddenly
she smells like an animal --
an uneasy feeling.

152 - 1955

THE ASAHI TANKA COLUMN (Poems 153-155)

Their urge to speak
held back so long,
it's in their poems now:
poets of newspaper tanka,
many with women's names.

153 - 1955

Groping to find words
for what boiled inside her,
breathlessly
she wrote it down:
I flinch before this tanka.

154 - 1955

I hear
their pleading, stammering
voices:
moved, I pause and gaze
at the clumsy handwriting.

155 - 1955

My mind
settles when my pencil is
sharpened;
I will discard anything
unnecessary left in me.

156 - 1957

She sleeps
during the day and grows
while she sleeps.
Flower and animal live
as one in my young girl.

157 - 1957

The Crown Prince's wedding: April 10 (March 3 by the old calendar).

Wings
moist with morning dew
a butterfly
wavers, ready to soar
into the azure sky.

158 - 1959

My lady
takes for her wedding present
one hundred of her tanka
filled with the thoughts,
feelings, of a young woman. [52]

159 - 1959

Mirrored
against the lapis lazuli sky
my daughter rides a horse
over the far swell of
Bluebell Hill. [53]

160 - 1959

POEMS 1960-68

At the window
of our house, to be inherited
again by a woman,
my daughter's face and mine
overlap in the morning mirror. [54]

161 - 1960

"Leave
all daily affairs to me and
write tanka" --
at the hospital I read
my daughter Izumi's words. [55]

162 - 1960

Thunder roars,
cracks in my secret cleft;
there is
a person about whom I think
"Die."

163 - 1961

As I wonder
what my daughter thinks
secretly tonight,
the snowy path of Narayama
appears in my mind. [56]

164 - 1961

The first day
I resolve to live life
for myself
I see the sun, a solid ball
blazing intensely.

165 - 1961

Each and
every gray hair of mine
glows
in seven colors;
my youth resurrects.

166 - 1961

Izumi, my daughter, had a serious car accident and has been hospitalized over two months. She is betrothed while still in her hospital bed.

My daughter
finally is with the person
she was destined
to meet; I am left empty
as an egg-shell.

167 - 1962

With my consent
my daughter is leaving me
to marry --
happy as I am, something
close to hate grows in me.

168 - 1962

For her wedding
my daughter sews late:
wide awake,
on this side of the sliding door,
I listen.

169 - 1962

I give
my only daughter
into his hands --
what pledges did we make
in our previous lives? [57]

170 - 1962

Each day
collecting new and
pretty things,
whatever she fancies,
my girl bundles them away.

171 - 1962

This peace and
too immense contentment
in my heart --
am I getting old?
I sense danger.

172 - 1962

When my heart
rebels and refuses
to grow old,
I push my children away
and sharpen my nails.

173 - 1962

AS I REFLECT ON MY PATH OF HALF A CENTURY
(Poems 174-176)

I have travelled
this path for half a century
revering
the words of my teacher,
"Be broad and deep and yourself." [58]

174 - 1962

"Raise
a rebellion," this order
was given me,
but I turned away;
I was thirty then. [59]

175 - 1962

Gushing
from my heart, hatred
against violence
drenched my whole being: that day
I listened to my living blood.

176 - 1962

Leaving for our trip to southern Japan.

Cherry
blossoms will soon open
from south to north
along the bow-shaped islands of Japan
washed by the eastern sea.

177 - 1963

While convalescing at Hayama. [60]

Being a woman is sad.
I hear that while laying eggs
sea turtles
shed large teardrops
onto the sands.

178 - 1963

My body
experienced in child-bearing
echoes
my daughter's pregnancy,
nearing its end.

179 - 1963

My daughter Izumi bore a baby girl on July 26, 1963. I found my first grandchild, Yukari, in a glass incubator in the room for premature infants at the Kantō Teishin Hospital.

Many days and
nights the baby fights
a tug of war
with the world of death.
When can I hug her?

180 - 1963

The baby
soon after birth
meets
the first spring snow;
it gleams in her eyes.

181 - 1964

With dry breasts,
but heart painfully
overflowing,
my body aches as I hold
this child in my arms.

182 - 1964

I strain
to care for the baby
day and night --
parts of my body
long forgotten move again.

183 - 1964

Sighing
heavily at midnight
I wonder,
"Has my dead daughter's spirit
been reborn in this child?"

184 - 1964

Aloud
I say, "My dead daughter
is aunt
to this child," -- but
it does not fit; I am sad.

185 - 1964

The days
of my life slide away
more and more quickly.
The baby will live on,
pass me by.

186 - 1964

Separated
from my dearest one,
my old age
turns rough and harsh --
I listen to the wind.

187 - 1965

Day after day
I yearn for my grandchild,
not able to turn into
a demon of attachment
or even a peaceful old woman. [61]

188 - 1966

MY TRIP TO EUROPE DRAWS NEAR (Poems 189-190)

As I feel
lonely, I peel a pear
and eat it.
The flesh is so much
like a little child's.

189 - 1967

In her coffin
we put foreign money;
may her soul fly
over the lands she can never
in the flesh visit again. [62]

190 - 1967

Forever
I'll remember that sky,
red as madder,
dawning over Rome --
soon I'll meet the child I love.

191 - 1967

STUDENT RIOT AT TOKYO UNIVERSITY (Poems 192-193) [63]

She, too, must
have wished to shout and rebel.
But not able
to break out, my daughter died --
her face returns to my mind.

192 - 1968

After thinking intensely,
my daughter said,
"I wish I could glide
through the roads in the sky
with balloons in my hands."

193 - 1968

POEMS 1970-76

Mountain birds
gather for the red *uwamizuzakura*
berries.
Now they come for regular
morning and evening meals. [64]

194 - 1970

My grandchild will return to Japan soon.

Puffing
puffing on the dandelion fluff
I walked
with the child in the spring light.
Soon we'll be warm in the sun again.

195 - 1971

A NEW MOON

Walked on
by man the lunar surface
remains clear
to my eyes. How young
and slender this crescent.

196 - 1971

ALONE AT MIDNIGHT (Poems 197-198)

Enraged
by something in the day,
late at night
I free my heart, watching
sword battles on TV.

197 - 1971

I follow
a fleeing villain
on the TV screen,
suddenly wishing for
his safe escape.

198 - 1971

"To love so much,
and be hurt so much":
at seventy
I learn this truth.
It sinks into my body. [65]

199 - 1971

She will not say,
"I want to see you," but tries
to make me say it.
My grandchild, eight years old,
knows love's tricks.

200 - 1971

On the sudden death of Kawabata Yasunari.

Do you tell me
to go on without your help?
Your words
about my poems
live in me yet. [66]

201 - 1972

I will benefit
even in my senile days;
my body is
a laboratory table
for testing my poems.

202 - 1972

In 1973, after observing the thirtieth anniversary of my mother's death.

The pine soars
on this cloudy day --
do I hear
my dead mother's soul
whispering?

203 - 1973

Why was I
unaware of it? Immense
is my remorse:
I, a stupendous fool,
a grandmother, cry aloud. [67]

204 - 1973

On the day I meet my granddaughter before she leaves for Geneva.

Love terms
in popular songs, usually
hateful to me,
sung by granddaughter
make me cry.

205 - 1974

"Have this,"
I say to the girl in my vision.
Juice keeps dripping
as all alone I peel a pear
on a cold night.

206 - 1975

This year
blossoms fill the sky;
I planted
those young mountain cherries
for my granddaughter to see.

207 - 1975

THE LILY HAS BLOOMED (Poems 208-209)

Father's deathday:
the lily opens its second flower.
Suddenly
I hear him calling,
"Come and look."

208 - 1975

My hair washed,
spread to the waist, billows
in the wind:
I gaze with my father
at the garden's radiant flowers.

209 - 1975

This morning
I feel out of touch:
I dreamed
of my grandchild sunk in thought
in a big transparent box.

210 - 1975

With the single desire
to behold her I flew
across the sky;
I did not see her
but must return. [68]

211 - 1975

A studio chair
pushed to one side,
dark lumps
of clay lie on the floor --
faces about to emerge. [69]

212 - 1975

The greater
her buoyance, the deeper
the wound
she inflicted on her mother.
Today my daughter truly shines.

213 - 1976

Pain
stops for a while, then
emptiness
unbearable; the proof
of my being is gone.

214 - 1976

I share food
with mountain birds.
The fruit and
roots nourish my body,
days and nights now peaceful.

215 - 1976

Potatoes
lie on the ground nodding
to each other,
the large ones silent
the small speaking aloud.

216 - 1976

Each time
I drink cow's milk, sharing
with the calves,
I recall my grandchild
in the days I prepared her milk.

217 - 1976

POEMS 1972-78

This year
my beloved girl comes home
crossing the seas,
her youthful body wrapped
in ocean fragrance.

218 - 1977

THE STORM OF BLOSSOMS (Poems 219-229) [70]

Blossom storm:
their shadows mingle, overlap
and cluster
with petals I have seen
in the many past springs of my life.

219 - 1977

Some deepen
in purple, some glow
in crimson,
brief as the tinkling of beads
blossoms storm through the dusk.

220 - 1977

Blossoms
scatter, mingle, and storm
in the sky
where the wind blows ceaselessly,
now and then avalanches of flowers.

221 - 1977

Blossoms
upon blossoms; from far away
flowers
come to my eyes, and flowers
in my dreams, too.

222 - 1977

Having lived
through illness I meet spring;
feeble, aged,
emaciated, I feel beaten
by the vibrant flowers.

223 - 1977

Full of pain,
my body crouches on the earth.
Yet it yearns to soar
into the sky on the day
when cherry blossoms storm.

224 - 1977

Blossoms seem
to storm and fall straight
to earth;
mist of flowers in the air
envelop sky and man.

225 - 1977

Blossoms,
slightly paler this year,
recall
the more brilliant beauty
of many other springs.

226 - 1977

The bright flowers
in the back of my eye
scatter and
mingle with the paler blossoms
storming now before me.

227 - 1977

Light and shadows
flicker through clustering blossoms.
Suddenly storming,
the flowers tumble in torrents --
painful splendor.

228 - 1977

As I look back
at the dark world I have seen,
how unreal
that flowers are blooming
and the moon, too, is full.

229 - 1977

LINGERING BLOSSOMS DANCE IN FRENZY (Poems 230-233) [71]

Flowers
of this year penetrate
my eye, sink
into my mind, pierce
my ailing stomach.

230 - 1977

My body filled
with pains, dreams linger
as days pass
with scattering blossoms
driven from nowhere.

231 - 1977

Blossoms
dance in a frenzy:
a snowstorm of flowers
by the playful wind
helplessly scattered.

232 - 1977

I say to myself,
"Still so many blossoms
on the treetops;"
I watch them fall and
swirl up again to their branches.

233 - 1977

I've been shown
the x-ray of my stomach;
spring advances
with white flowers of pears,
azaleas, lilies of the valley.

234 - 1977

My grandchild
is flying over the North Pole.
When our eyes meet
I shall be consumed
by aurora-blue flames.

235 - 1977

Carried
by the wind, the scent
of flowers
visits me, but not a sign
of my precious child.

236 - 1977

Suddenly
my beloved girl looks away
after a glance
at me from behind the clouds.
My dream broken, I wake up.

237 - 1977

I am together
with you, my dearest one.
But why is my love
for you still unfulfilled?
What is this longing?

238 - 1977

Although we share
the same blood, my dearest child
is inaccessible.
I, the mother of her mother, am ill,
worn with love for her.

239 - 1978

THE COLOR VIOLET (Poems 240-246)

Spring fragrance
hovers faintly
as dusk falls,
absorbing the earth
in the color violet.

240 - 1978

Darkness
deepens and I keep
wondering
what is its color? --
violet flashes into my mind.

241 - 1978

Dusk
spreads its hues,
dark and pale
slowly dissolves
into violet.

242 - 1978

Alive,
I see again sky and earth
wavering
in violet color
as the day closes.

243 - 1978

Purple at first,
dusk deepens
until all is black:
watching the colors shifting,
I merge into the darkness.

244 - 1978

Breathing
in the darkness,
totally wrapped
in the color violet,
I am alive.

245 - 1978

To be alive,
this great thing,
is now one
and the same as the color
violet purple.

246 - 1978

Chronology
and
Commentary

Chronology

1898 Gotō Miyoko born in Tokyo.

1908 Began reading the Bible. Baptized in August.

1911 Studied the poems of Emperor Meiji and Empress Dowager Shōken.

1912 Became a pupil of Ogasawara Seimu, the master of the Ogasawara Style rules of etiquette of the 600-year-old tradition.

1914 Studied classical Japanese literature at the Institute of Japanese. Began reading *The Tale of Genji* and read twenty or so volumes of the *Complete Works of Classical Japanese Literature* in the family library.

1915 Became a pupil of Sasaki Nobutsuna; her career as a tanka poet began.

1916 Taught Japanese at Seiei Girls' School. Had her first experience of the frenzied state of creativity that she later called "the demon's visit," resulting in dozens of tanka written in one night.

1919 Obtained a primary-school teaching certificate. Taught at Bankō Girls' School established and directed by her mother.

1923 Obtained a middle-school teaching certificate in Japanese.

1924 Became an auditor at Tokyo University. Joined Tokyo University Tanka Society and met Ishigure Shigeru.

1925 May, Miyoko and Shigeru married.

1926 April, Hitomi born.

1928 Joined the League of Newly Rising Tanka Poets led by Shigeru. Withdrew from the tanka society of her teacher Sasaki Nobutsuna, which published the influential journal, *The Flower of the Heart*.

1929 March, joined the *Spearhead*, a magazine founded by Shigeru and his friends. April, moved to Osaka as Shigeru became assistant professor at Osaka University of Commerce. July, joined the Association of Proletarian Tanka Poets. Disobeyed

an order "Raise a rebellion" and left the association.
Gave up writing tanka.

1931   April, left for London with Shigeru on his study abroad.

1932   Spent the summer in Newtown in Wales, where Shigeru was engaged in his research on Robert Owen. Visited Scotland on the way back to London.

1933   January, Shigeru left for Berlin for three months of research. Miyoko stayed in London with her daughter Hitomi, and began writing tanka again. Spent the whole month of May in Paris. Visited Switzerland and Italy before boarding a ship at Naples bound for Japan. Back in Japan, she returned to publishing in *The Flower of the Heart*.

1935   July, her father died.

1936   Her first book of tanka, *The Warm Current*, published.

1937   May, second daughter, Izumi, was born.

1938   Shigeru and Miyoko founded a tanka magazine, *The Arrival of Spring*.

1942   August, death of her father-in-law, Ishigure Chimata. October, *Women's Guide for Composing Tanka* published.

1943   March, her mother died. Became owner and director of Bankō Girls' School.

1944   Shigeru resigned from his university post to join Miyoko in Tokyo. Hitomi entered Tokyo Women's Higher Normal School.

1945   Under the ordinance of student labor mobilization Hitomi and her schoolmates worked in an aeroplane manufacturing factory in Nagoya.

1946   April, second collection of her tanka, *On the Hill*, published. May, *The Arrival of Spring* resumed its publication after two years' suspension during the war. Studied English poetry.

1948   Hitomi entered Tokyo University. While remaining principal of Bankō Girls' School, Miyoko again became an auditor at the same university and attended lectures on Buddhism for two years. Joined the weekly seminar on *The Tale of Genji* conducted by Ikeda Kikan. There met the young scholar who was later to make the definitive translation of *The Tale of Genji*, Edward Seidensticker. Attended with Hitomi the lectures by Edmund Blunden, visiting poet from England.

1949   Became a research student at Tokyo University. Appointed a lecturer of Senshū University. Founded, with other women poets, *Women's Tanka*.

1950   January, Hitomi died. March, the severe blow of Hitomi's sudden death and financial difficulties led to the closing of Bankō Girls' School. Became a professor of Senshū University (held the position till 1968). October, her fourth collected tanka, *The Wind*, published.

1951   Miyoko was ill for most of this year. Shigeru became a professor of the Tokyo University of Foreign Languages.

1952   March, the delayed third collection of her tanka, *Fire and Snow*, published. October, *How to Compose Tanka*, published.

1953   July, to commemorate the third anniversary of Hitomi's death, *Tanka Poems of a Mother*, published.

1955   Became a selector for the Tanka Column of the *Asahi Newspaper*. She remained a dedicated judge for twenty-two years till the year of her death.

1957   September, the expanded new edition of *Tanka Poems of a Mother*, published; *My Tanka*, published.

1958   February, awarded Yomiuri Literary Prize for *Tanka Poems of a Mother: New Enlarged Edition*. Appointed a selector of tanka submitted for the New Year's Poetry Party held at the imperial court (served till 1965).

1959   January-March, gave a special intensive tanka instruction to Miss Shōda Michiko, now the Crown Princess of Japan. April, appointed her regular instructor in tanka. Spent the summer at the newly-built villa in Karuizawa.

1961   June, her fifth tanka collection, *I Am Alive*, published.

1962   July, Izumi seriously injured in a car accident. October, Izumi discharged from the hospital and married in December.

1963   July, granddaughter, Yukari, born prematurely. November, *The Collected Tanka Poems of Gotō Miyoko* published.

1967   December, made a Christmas visit to her granddaughter in Rome.

1968   April, appointed a professor of Sapporo University in Hokkaidō and flew there for monthly lectures. July, the sixth collection of tanka, *Time Difference*, published. September-November, Shigeru and Miyoko taught at the University of Hawaii as visiting professors.

1971   November, awarded by the Japanese government a Purple Ribbon Medal.

1972   November, gave a lecture on *The Tale of Genji* at the International Conference on Japanese Cultural Studies sponsored by the Japan PEN Club.

1973   November, the seventh tanka collection, *Falling Water*, published.

1974   Izumi divorced and later married a young sculptor.

1975   June, went with Shigeru on a European trip to celebrate their golden wedding. In Geneva they were unable to see their granddaughter by her father and his new wife. December, the 300th issue of *The Arrival of Spring*, published.

1977   January-March and June-August, hospitalized at the Ōtsuka Cancer Research Institute Hospital in Tokyo. Later in August while staying at Karuizawa, fell into a five-day coma caused by bleeding ulcers. October-December, again hospitalized. Despite her serious condition the year saw her extraordinarily creative, producing 142 tanka besides occasional lectures.

1978   January, after a three-month break, returned to work as a selector for the Asahi Tanka Column. February, wrote seven tanka under a general title, "The Color Violet," published in March. Towards the end of February, again hospitalized due to ulcer and liver complications. On February 26 fell into a coma. On February 28 the Crown Princess visited Miyoko at the hospital, but she did not revive until March 4th. On April 7 rejoiced to receive the cherry blossoms sent from the Crown Princess' garden. Died on April 15. December, the eighth tanka collection *The Storm of Blossoms*, published.

1979   April, *The Flower Clock*, the first collection of Miyoko's prose writings, published.

1983   April, *The Definitive Tanka Collection of Gotō Miyoko*, published.

Commentary

Early Years: 1898-1923

Gotō Miyoko was born (forty days prematurely) on July 12, 1898. Her father, Seitarō, professor of biology of the First Higher School in Tokyo, later taught at Tokyo University where he became a professor emeritus in 1928. Her mother, Chiyotsuchi, one of the first graduates of the renowned Meiji Girls' School, was a teacher at her Alma Mater at the time of Miyoko's birth.

The families of both Seitarō and Chiyotsuchi belonged to the ex-samurai class, Seitarō's father being a former retainer of the Chōshū clan, and Chiyotsuchi's of the Saga clan. The fiefs of both clans were in the far western region of Japan from which the leaders of anti-*bakufu* movement emerged to bring about the Meiji Restoration in 1868. After the total abolition of the hereditary stipend system upon which the clansmen of feudal Japan depended, most of the ex-military class faced severe financial difficulties as they tried, often unsuccessfully, to become farmers or merchants. [72] Both of Miyoko's grandfathers were among the lucky minority who managed to become functionaries in the new westernized government. Seitarō's father became an official of the Mint Bureau in Osaka; Chiyotsuchi's, a naval officer who attained the rank of captain.

Seitarō learned English from his father at the age of six and entered Osaka English School at thirteen. Before he began specializing in biology at Tokyo University, he studied for two years, 1882-1884, under Niishima Jō (1843-1890) at Dōshisha English School founded in 1875 by this important Christian educator. Seitarō's parents were Christians and he was baptized when he was fourteen.

Chiyotsuchi also received the new liberal education promoted by the intellectuals who led Japan's modernization under the slogan "Civilization and Enlightenment." English was considered a tool for learning and at her school English textbooks were used for such subjects as geography, history, and arithmetic. Thus, both Miyoko's parents were fluent in English and in her childhood English was frequently spoken at home.

The Meiji Girls' School, dedicated to educating Japanese women through Christian ideals, was established in 1885. Instead of conferring diplomas it chose to avoid the government-approved curricula designed to produce obedient housewives. Pioneers of the women's movement in Japan were helped by its exceptionally high standards and a liberal curriculum that emphasized spiritual and economic independence for women. Nogami Yaeko (1885-1985), a 1906 graduate of the school and a distinguished novelist, reminisces:

"If I had spent my school life at any other institution, I would not be what I am now. Especially, my way of thinking, I believe, was fostered at that school. What we might call 'idealism' had great weight. Although I would not say that we were free from authorities in the society, opinions of the world, conventions, and formalities, we came to develop our way of thinking unaffected by these." [73]

She also reports that there were no examinations, and that during her six years at the school the Imperial Rescript on Education was never read, as was customary elsewhere, to the students. [74] Her school years correspond to Miyoko's early girlhood; on Miyoko's death in 1978 Yaeko wrote the poem "Recollections;" its first stanza:

Miyoko-chan,
those days now far distant
in the *kunugi* grove of Sugamo
with a big sister, Okiyo-san of the Iwamotos,
Tami-chan, Shinko-chan, Yocchan of Yutanis,

all together,
picking acorns,
gathering wild flowers,
you were having great fun.
A young girl of those days;
that is my fondest memory of you. [75]

When after a fire the school was moved from its central location, Kudan, to Sugamo on the western outskirts of Tokyo, Miyoko's parents built a new house adjacent to it, or as Miyoko puts it, "on its campus." Sugamo in 1903 was still a woody suburb of Tokyo. In the fictionalized episodic accounts of her childhood, "Kurai me" (Dark Bud) posthumously collected in *The Flower Clock*, Miyoko in her late twenties wrote a vivid description of the pastoral surroundings in 1905:

Their house was surrounded by thickets of trees on the west and south sides, and beyond them there was a bamboo grove separating the house from the building of Mciji Girls' School. They had a distant view of Mt. Fuji from a field just behind the house. On the east just one house stood between her grandmother's and a street. She was planning to have a new house built on the spacious lot. The tea fields stretched from this area to the school dormitory. There was an expansive open space where children played.

Flowers spread all over the tree thickets: blooming *shidome* in spring and tiny lily-shaped blossoms in autumn. [76] Miyoko gazed at the blossoms, filled with a strange feeling and wondering if they were the lilies of the field in the passage of the Bible she had often heard: "Consider the lilies of the field, how they grow; ... That even Solomon in all his glory was not arrayed like one of these." On summer evenings pure white blossoms of railway grass covered the vacant lot as well as the spaces between the tea-fields. [77] Children snapped off the flowers and threw them over one another (HD, p. 31).

The Meiji Girls' School played an important role in the development of modern Japanese literature. Iwamoto Yoshiharu (1863-1942), who helped start the school in 1885 and later headed it, had launched, in 1884, *Jogakuzasshi* (*Magazine of Women's Learning*), the first periodical of significance promoting the same ideals as those held at the school. Two major modern Japanese writers, Shimazaki Tōson (1872-1943) and Kitamura Tōkoku (1868-1894) began their careers on this journal and taught at Iwamoto's school in the mid 1890s. In 1893 these two and their colleagues formed a new monthly, *Bungakukai* (*Literary World*), which became the center of the early Romantic movement in Meiji Japan. Though she was born too late to be taught by these literary figures, young Miyoko obviously was nurtured by their spirit of idealism.

When she reached school age in 1905, Miyoko, instead of attending a local school, was taught calligraphy by her grandmother and other subjects by her mother and the teachers and senior students of Meiji Girls' School. The following year she skipped two grades and was enrolled in the fourth at a local school. After her completion in 1909 of the newly reformed primary education her academic career remained irregular.

Growing up in an environment permeated with Christian idealism, Miyoko at the age of nine was led to the Bible by, she says, a spontaneous urge. The text was written in difficult classical Japanese so she slowly and carefully read a couple of lines a day. Her parents, worried by the serious daily studies of this fragile child, were badly frightened when Miyoko fell seriously ill; but, according to her own words, she was not afraid of death rather she felt she had always before her a light which she believed to be the light of Paradise. In August of this same year, 1908, she was baptized; her recovery the next month seemed to the family a miracle (HD, p. 68).

Miyoko says of her experience with Scripture:

> Though I was not conscious of it, this beginning of my life with books affected my later attitude towards reading. Years later I became aware that reading could never be casual to me. Between my daily life and whatever I read there was always a link so serious as to appear foolish to others. Any book lacking this link did not interest me enough even to look at (HD, pp. 68-69).

In the same essay we also learn that the ten-year-old Miyoko tried to fuse into her everyday life what her heart grasped from the words in the Bible.

In "Dark Bud" we also have, however, an anecdote that reveals a somewhat blasphemous little Miyoko:

> "From him that hath not shall be taken away even that which he hath": one day this passage in the Bible came up in a family conversation. Miyoko [sic] strained her ears to understand its meaning: those who are weak and those who are evil are forced to greater wrongdoings; those who are poor get poorer and are reduced even to robbery---
>
> When Miyoko's child mind began to have a vague understanding of what they were talking about, she was shocked and impatiently asked:
>
> "Mother, does God punish even people like them?"
>
> "Yes, of course if they do wrong."
>
> "Does He punish them, even though they are so poor and

> pitiful? Does He do such a cruel thing?"
>
> Miyoko suddenly shouted, her face distorted by sobs:
>
> "Then we'll kill Him, if He is such a God!"
>
> Her parents looked at each other, surprised by these violent words, the first words of blasphemy against God by the child who would think it a great sin to go against even the most casual words of her parents (HD, p. 26).

This anecdote appears in the chapter symbolically entitled "Fire"; it refers to a "tiny, faint flame ready to blaze" hidden in Miyoko aged seven or eight (HD, p. 25).

More doubts soon grew. At thirteen Miyoko was particularly annoyed by such passages as: "I the Lord thy God am a jealous God, visiting the iniquity of the fathers upon the children unto the third and fourth generation of them that hate me." She determined to side with those afflicted by this revengeful God.

Miyoko's adolescent experiences with the Bible illuminate the quintessence of her poetry: while the serious-minded Miyoko gives her poems straightforward realistic voices, the power of her passion leads the reader beyond ordinary understanding as her sharp, often daring insights create intense moments. Marvelous reflections of the environment in which she was brought up, her poems are also genetically rooted: the idealistic and passionate Miyoko seems to reflect her mother, a devoted educator, while her independent discerning mind is a legacy of her father, a distinguished scientist. Though its intensity varied, the flame kept burning in Miyoko as wife, mother, grandmother, teacher, school principal, proletarian tanka poet, invalid, judge for a newspaper tanka column, and tanka teacher to the Crown Princess.

After the Meiji Girls' School closed in 1910 Miyoko attended a private school where her mother began to put Iwamoto's principles into practice. During the two years at her mother's school she was taught composition by Nogami Yaeko, and read for the first time the tanka of Emperor Meiji and his consort (Empress Dowager Shōken). Their poems induced in her a desire to write "*makoto no uta*," poems that are a sincere expression of one's thoughts and feelings. The lasting impact of these imperial poems is revealed in Miyoko's tanka as well as essays written in her mid-sixties.

Miyoko's initiation into tanka actually came a year earlier through a popular game called "*Hyakunin'isshu*" (The Hundred Poems by One Hundred Poets), played during New Year's holidays. The game consists of one hundred cards, each giving the closing half of a famous tanka from the seventh to the thirteenth centuries. In order to pick up the cards as fast as possible while the poems are recited, children memorize the tanka without really comprehending them, but the rhythm is captivating. Miyoko's unusually strong fascination with this rhythm was crucial to her future development as a tanka poet. She writes in an essay "*Uta no hajime*" (My Beginning with Tanka):

> Tanka entered me with a rhythm that thoroughly permeated my heart; a rhythm belonging to a world still unknown to me yet remembered for centuries by the blood that also runs in me (HD, p. 244).

Secret attempts at tanka, "imitations of old masters" in Miyoko's words, now appeared in her diaries and notebooks; then her encounter with the poems of Emperor Meiji and Empress Dowager Shōken helped her own voice to emerge.

Miyoko's father also contributed in indirect and subtle ways. He loved nature and had a spacious garden of blooming plants; in the spring of 1913, when she was fourteen, Miyoko opened to the beauty of nature, especially the unearthly splendor of cherry blossoms, and poems came to fill her notebooks.

In 1914, Miyoko began to prepare for a teacher's license examinations: though her irregular schooling did not qualify her for the profession, she had decided even as a small girl to become a teacher. In 1915 she took the official license examinations in four subjects, passing them with distinction.

September 10th of the same year marked the beginning of Miyoko's formal career as a tanka poet: abiding by the traditional practice of coming under some established poet's tuition, Miyoko became a disciple of Sasaki Nobutsuna (1872-1963), a respected scholar of classical Japanese poetry and a poet who had founded in 1898 an influential tanka magazine, *Kokoro no hana* (*Flower of the Heart*). Her weekly lessons with him were stimulating and Miyoko later recalled that poems flowed out of her as if pushed by an inexplicable surge of energy. Throughout her life she often experienced this frenzied state of mind, which she describes as a "demon's visit" (*oni ga kuru*), at varying intervals -- "small waves once a month and big ones once a year or a few years" (HD, p. 246).

Miyoko finally obtained her teaching certificate in 1919 and began to teach at the Bankō Girls' School, newly founded by her mother. Four years later, in 1923 she took the secondary school teacher's license that qualified her to attend lectures at a university, though only as an auditor -- in those days women were not yet admitted as regular students. Seven months after the great 1924 earthquake in Tokyo, Miyoko began her post-secondary education in a makeshift building at Tokyo University. In May she joined the Tokyo University Tanka Society and met Ishigure Shigeru (1900-), a young scholar of economics and the third son of Ishigure Chimata (1869-1942), well-known tanka poet and the editor of her teacher's magazine, *Flower of the Heart*.

In the decade after becoming a student of Sasaki Nobutsuna in 1915, she wrote nearly 4000 poems. She chose only eighty-three of these adolescent works for her first published tanka collection in 1936. Though the tanka of this period are often vague and repetitious they do reflect the sincerity and seriousness as well as the keen poetic sensitivity of the budding poet:

In the past
I told God everything
I felt
and thought. My poems
are truly my prayers. [78]

arishi hi wa
kami ni nagekishi
omoi nari
waga uta wa tada
inori ni onaji

1 - 1921

The appeal of this tanka in the original depends largely on its rhythmic flow. As the transliteration shows the poem is rich in echoing sounds: "*i*" is predominant in the first three lines and repeated in the final; "*ri*" occurs in the first, third and sixth lines, contributing to structural unity; and "*a*" is heard six times in the seven-syllable fourth line, placing the focus of this tanka on "*waga uta*" or "my poems." This rhythm helps to convey the earnestness the young Miyoko brought to writing poetry.

In "My Beginning with Tanka" Miyoko relates an episode pertinent not only to this tanka but also to her entire life as a poet. About six months after she started her lessons with Sasaki Nobutsuna, her teacher asked whether she was a Christian. She was at a loss how to answer. At the next session she gave him an essay responding to his question. Reading it he said quietly, "I believe that if we put ourselves deeply into something, say, tanka, the same strength we gain through religion will be born in us" (HD, p. 247). When she heard these words Miyoko felt a profound joy and peace of mind; she resolved to devote her life to tanka. Poetry became and remained her religion, often rescuing her from the depths of almost inconsolable sorrow.

POEMS 1924-30 [79]

Miyoko's poetry from this period is given here in two parts: "Early Tanka" (1924-28), and "In One Stage of My Life" (1929-30).

"Early Tanka" centers on Miyoko's personal life, her engagement to Ishigure Shigeru, marriage, intimate feelings about her first child.

The poems of "In One Stage of My Life" are unique among the entire body of Miyoko's work -- they are seriously concerned with the underprivileged working class, and daringly experimental in style.

EARLY TANKA (1924-28)

Shigeru and Miyoko were engaged in November of 1924 and married in May of the following year. Since Miyoko's parents did not have sons, Miyoko's husband followed Japanese custom and assumed her family surname as his own. For a while, however, Shigeru continued to use his original surname on some of his publications.

After marriage Miyoko continued teaching at her mother's school, maintained her position as an auditor at Tokyo University, and wrote tanka.

Though she was originally "annoyed with the possibility of becoming pregnant," (HD, p. 93) in the autumn of 1925 her attitude changed when she felt movement in her womb. Struck with a combination of surprise and joy she wrote tanka about the experience. She "secretly felt apprehensive and even shy about writing tanka on this subject" (HD, p. 93) because tanka was traditionally restrained and reserved about such intimate physical things. In the history of tanka, and Japanese poetry in general, no poet had ever before composed a poem on fetal movement. Kawada Jun (1882-1966), an important member of the *Flower of the Heart*, described Miyoko's poem as "the first step into an unexplored field." [80]

Her first child was born on April 22, 1926. Despite her mother's suggestion that she continue teaching Miyoko gave up all activities except writing tanka in order to devote herself to the baby. During this time a wonderful harmony existed between her poetic and maternal activities: the more intense her commitment to her child, the more powerful her poems became. This seems the first step towards Miyoko's mature style in which firm realism and powerful emotion are united by rhythmic spontaneity.

The baby was named Hitomi, "pupil of the eye." Twenty-three years later, one year before Hitomi's sudden death, Miyoko used the English expression: "the apple of my eye" to describe how much this daughter meant to her (TGMZ, p. 216; see poem 118).

"Gazing," a dominant motif of Miyoko's poems of this early period, but her experience of gazing at the baby is not expressed as one of maternal wonder. From the very beginning there is an intense, even passionate relationship. (See poem 8)

In the essay: "Ninen tatte" (Two Years After [Hitomi's Death], written c. 1952), Miyoko says:

> ... on the second night after her birth, Hitomi cried so much ... that she was brought into my bed by her nurse. But the nurse soon fell asleep, and so, all night I had the secret joy of hugging my daughter for the first time with nobody coming between us.
>
> As if I now openly had my first meeting with someone whom I have been intensely longing for, I held tight in my arms the baby whose eyes were not yet open, with tears flowing on my cheeks (HD, p. 94).

In her tanka Miyoko sees herself mirrored in this baby, a reflection that implies more than mere facial resemblance.

As she matured as poet and mother, Miyoko developed a subtle, complex psychological approach to the mother and child relationship. In her tanka she questions her uncertainty about her overprotectiveness, and her ambivalence about scolding the child, and how her vision of reality was transformed by the child's drawing of Hanare Hill (landmark in a fashionable summer resort north of Tokyo).

During this time, Miyoko also experienced powerful ideological stimulation from her husband. Recalling the years immediately after their marriage, she writes: "Dazzled by the new world opened to me by my husband day after day, I lived a breathless life. Even though I did not produce many tanka (under this influence), my outlook seemed to have gone through a complete change" (TGMZ, p. 568).

Her husband's influence helped Miyoko to move beyond the naivete and vagueness that characterize many poems written before her marriage.

IN ONE STAGE OF MY LIFE (1929-30)

The mid-1920's brought a rebellion against the tradition of tanka. In early 1926 a group of poets dissociated themselves from the conservative tanka establishments to form a new tanka society that advocated the use of common, everyday language in composing tanka.

During the following year, when Japan experienced a serious collapse of the banking system three years prior to the world-wide depression of the 1930's, two tanka poets specializing in economics composed articles on proletarian tanka and initiated a tanka revolution. Writing in 1983, Shino Hiroshi emphasizes the importance of this new movement and of poets who were aware of the economic crises latent in their capitalistic society. [81]

In January of 1927, Shigeru completed the outline of his own polemical criticism *Tanka kakushin no shinten* (*The Progress of Tanka Revolution*) which was serialized in the "*Tanka zasshi*" (*The Tanka Magazine*) from February to November 1928. [82] In it he applied the theory of dialectic materialism to the examination of contemporary tanka.

Saitō Mokichi (1882-1953), leader of Araragi, the most influential tanka society of the period, severely attacked Shigeru's Marxist approach. But Shigeru's articles represented a young generation of tanka poets who were dissatisfied with the powerful master-poet system of conservative tanka groups. A new epoch in the history of modern tanka had opened.

In September 1928 a new tanka league was formed with Shigeru as one of its leaders: Shinkō Kajin Remmei (League of Newly Rising Tanka Poets). Some of it's slogans were: "United front for revolutionary movement," "Abandonment of the contradictions of content and form," and "Persistent self-criticism." [83] Formation of the league marked the end of the tanka of the Taishō era (1912-25) which had been dominated by the Araragi School. Miyoko, an enthusiastic follower of her husband's new poetic ideals, joined the League.

The new association was composed of poets with two different objectives: those solely concerned about the promotion of tanka dealing with working class, others aiming at a wider range of poetic innovation, including colloquial tanka (which used everyday words rather than the old traditional language). This difference led to so much internal conflict that some of the league's members founded Musansha Kajin Remmei (League of Proletarian Tanka Poets), Japan's first organization of proletarian poets. Shigeru's league was disbanded in December, 1928, only three months after its formation.

Three months later, in March of 1929, Shigeru and his friends started a new tanka magazine: *Sentan (The Spearhead)*. Poems 16, 19 and 20 are among Miyoko's tanka published in its first issue. The *Spearhead* was discontinued four months later.

At this same time the League of Proletarian Tanka Poets grew into a larger society: Provetaria Kajin Dōmei (Association of Proletarian

Tanka Poets). Shigeru, disillusioned with the internal strife in the revolutionary tanka movement, chose to distance himself.

Miyoko joined the Association and published her new experimental tanka in its periodical: *Tanka sensen* (*The Tanka Battleline*), a publication succeeded by *Tanka zen'ei* (*The Tanka Avant-garde*). When this group published *Provetaria tanka shū* (*Collection of Proletarian Tanka*) in 1930, eleven of Miyoko's tanka were included -- pieces marked by stark realism, rough language, harsh rhythm. They comprised two units: the first dealt with the hardships and frustrations of factory women, the second with draftees who become insane (possibly due to the cruelty of the army). The first group was titled: "Set Women's Hearts on Fire." The title of the second group is not clear because three of the seven characters in the title were suppressed by the censor. Other suppressed characters indicate the censorship was due to some implied criticism of the army. [84]

In 1929, Miyoko received a mysterious note. Its exact source is unknown, but she speculated that it came from the proletarian poets' association and was designed to test her devotion to the movement. It ordered her "to raise a rebellion." Miyoko left the group instead; she did not wish to have any part of physical violence for the cause of a tanka revolution (see poems 175 and 176).

Despite the mystery surrounding the note Miyoko regarded her refusal to act as a kind of betrayal of her proletarian associates and stopped publishing tanka until 1933. She felt that "for a person to whom tanka is life, giving up tanka would be equal to suicide" and she wished to express her deep sense of shame through this form of self-immolation (TGMZ, p. 85).

This turbulent phase of her life corresponds to the height of the proletarian movements in other genres of modern Japanese literature. Miyoko referred to this period as "In One Stage of My Life," and determined to make a completely fresh start, "destroying whatever she had already learned about tanka" (TGMZ, p. 84).

New subjects entered her poems, which were written in the vernacular and often contained harsh self-criticism. Their colloquial syntax violated traditional syllabic rhythm, and she chose to exceed the regular thirty-one syllables with anything from two to nineteen. Consequently they cannot be translated into the five-line form. Since they share a common structural feature - they can usually be divided into two parts, the division falling at about the center of the poem - they are translated here into two lines.

Miyoko regarded this poetry as immature yet did not want it set aside as irregular, one-time-only pieces. Instead, she hoped it would prove to be the "flesh and blood" of her future poetic development (TGMZ, p. 84).

According to Shigeru, most of these tanka did not reflect direct contact with the subjects dealt with, but this does not mean Miyoko modeled them on other proletarian poems; they reflect her serious attempt to analyze her position as a member of the petite bourgeoisie and to put herself in the place of the underprivileged, just as Yamanoue no Okura of the eighth century did in his famous chōka: "Dialogue on Poverty."

POEMS 1931-39

These thirty poems were translated from *The Warm Current* and *On the Hill*. They can be divided into two parts: Poems composed abroad (1932-33); and Poems written at home (1935-39).

Most of the first section was written during Miyoko's stay in Europe and was later collected under the title: "Taiōkashō" (A Selection of Tanka Composed Abroad). A few of these poems apparently were composed after her return; one such piece in the chōka form is "Monsoon."

Chōka as a poetic form is perhaps older than tanka, though its popularity ceased after the eighth century. Chōka allows for the creation of a poetic narrative in the traditional pattern of alternating five and seven syllable lines (In "Monsoon" this rhythm is occasionally violated). Chōka end with an extra seven syllable line and are usually followed by one or more envoys (hanka) or short poems that take the same syllabic form as tanka and are used to sum up the content or emotion of the narrative. Tanka poets still use this form, taking advantage of its rhythmic structure (that does not require stanza breaks) and its unrestricted length. Miyoko wrote "Monsoon," the first chōka in her tanka collections, soon after she ceased her self-alienation from tanka, perhaps using the extended form to accent her deliverance.

The twenty-one poems in the second group, "Poems written at home," reflect major events in Miyoko's life: the death of her father (1935), the birth of her second daughter (1937), the outbreak of the Sino-Japanese War (1937), the founding of the Risshun Tanka Society and its journal: *The Arrival of Spring* (1938).

Despite this range of experiences Miyoko's poetic focus is still her response to her daughters: Izumi, in her infancy, and Hitomi, in her early teens.

Poems Composed Abroad (1932-33)

While studying at Tokyo University, Shigeru began his life-long work on Robert Owen (1771-1858), the pioneer of a co-operative movement who used socialist and philanthropist ideals to run cotton-spinning mills in Manchester, England. In 1931, Shigeru's research took him and his young family to England and Wales, and Miyoko hoped that her busy life abroad would help her to cut herself off completely from tanka.

During their second year away, Shigeru took a three-month research trip to Berlin and Miyoko stayed in London with Hitomi. Although she was trying to refrain from writing Miyoko began to jot down in her diary, poems filled with personal emotion and sensitive responses to whatever she encountered in her London life. Despite the pain it had brought her, Miyoko's proletarian concerns were still, as in her depiction of winter in Piccadilly, reflected in her art.

In 1933, before returning home, the Gotōs stayed in Paris for the month of May and frequented the Louvre. They also took a special train trip in Italy that covered the country, from north to south, in just a few days. Miyoko, impressed by the enduring tradition of Italian art, broke into a "cold sweat" thinking of how she had spoken out for "the abandonment of tradition" (TGMZ, p. 573).

When the family returned to Japan in 1933, the editor of *Tanka shinbun* (*The Tanka Newspaper*) invited Miyoko to contribute some poetry. After much hesitation about publishing again she managed to select several pieces from her diary and letters. Encouraged by her teacher, Sasaki Nubutsuna, she rejoined his society: Flower of the Heart.

POEMS WRITTEN AT HOME (1935-39).

Though the resurgence of her creativity is clear in the new tanka, and especially in "Monsoon," Miyoko's return to her career as a tanka poet was not smooth. She spent six-months trying to readjust to life in Japan, then was caught up in a chain of illnesses: pyelitis, appendicitis (in the autumn of 1934 she had an appendectomy) and towards the end of the year, diphtheria (see TGMZ, p. 538). In the early summer of the following year, her father fell ill. Miyoko left her home in Osaka and went to Tokyo to nurse him. He died July 20, 1935 from liver cancer.

The three poems concerning her father's death (45, 46 and 47) are from a group of seventeen tanka entitled "Having Lost My Father" found at the end of her first tanka collection, *The Warm Current*, published a year after his death.

Miyoko had been deeply attached to the brilliant, somewhat lonely scientist. She regretted the fact that he was not able to see her book: it was he who had supported her dream of being a poet; he was the one who had bought her *The Great Compendium of Japanese Poetry*, a collection of classical tanka from mythological times through the 15th century. Her fondness for him is reflected in many of her later poems.

In 1936, eleven years after Hitomi's birth, Miyoko got another chance to write about being an expectant mother. Her tanka about the second pregnancy show a mature ease with the experience; they also contain a rich sensuality as well as an enlightened objectivity that her early tanka on this subject lacked. (Compare poems 5 and 6 with poems 49, 51 and 52).

Her poetry in this period also reflected her sensitive observations of Hitomi, just going through puberty (poem 48).

Miyoko felt Hitomi was growing up with a hardiness that the poet herself lacked (poem 59) and she anticipated an eventual cleavage (poem 60). Her psychological approach to the mother-child relationship gained intensity and depth as Miyoko watched her daughter grow into womanhood.

Her poems about Hitomi brought tanka to another unexplored area of female experience: by subtly hinting at Hitomi's first menstrual cycle, Miyoko opened up another subject untouched in traditional tanka poetry (poems 64 and 65). [85]

In 1953, Miyoko reminisced about her maternal feelings during this time:

On May 1937 my second daughter was born. With a child in each arm I felt as if I had with me all the happiness and treasures of this world. Even during the severest war time I thought nothing could give me pain *as long as I did not lose my children* (TGMZ, p.577; italics by the translator).

The date in this quote corresponds to the beginning of the Sino-Japanese War, which broke out two months after her second daughter, Izumi, was born. As the war escalated, Miyoko's heart grew "restless and fettered/ by attachment" to the baby (poem 55). Her tanka expressed a strong determination to protect her children from deprivation. Miyoko felt she was "not far from" the "worlds of 'hungry spirits' and *ashura*," (references to two Buddhist terms: *gakidō* the path of hungry spirits and *shuradō* the path of *ashura*).

Gakidō and *shuradō* are two of the *rokudō* (six paths or worlds), the lowest of which is hell, and the highest of which is the world of 'heavenly beings' through which a soul eternally transmigrates. *Gakidō* (the path of hungry spirits) is the second lowest of the six; those who have fallen this far experience perpetual hunger because food here bursts into flame the moment it is touched.

The path of *ashura* or *shuradō*, is the fourth lowest. The term originates in the name of a spirit Buddhists consider arrogant and evil. It is abbreviated as *shura*, and the suffix *dō* (meaning world or realm) is added to it; *shuradō* represents an existence of constant strife.

In the midst of escalating war, Miyoko felt close to the worlds of perpetual hunger and constant strife. Haunted by these feelings she compares herself to Kishimojin (poem 56).

According to legend, Kishimojin was a ferocious demon who had five hundred offspring. In order to feed her children, she ate the infants of humans. Buddha, wanting to reform Kishimojin, hid her youngest child. Unable to find her baby she was beside herself with grief. Buddha admonished her: if she felt so distressed at the loss of just one child out of her five hundred she should understand the sorrows of the parents whose children she had eaten.

Miyoko's tanka of this period reveal a vacillation between happiness and anxiety, a fluctuation that anticipates an even stronger swing of moods in later work that reflects her increasingly complex relations with her daughters.

In May of 1938, Miyoko and Shigeru founded their tanka society, *Risshun (The Arrival of Spring)*. Referring to the twelve month span that began with Izumi's birth (in May of 1937) and ended with the founding of *The Arrival of Spring*, Miyoko remarked: "It is a period in which I searched myself, seeking to discover something about my own being" (TGMZ, p. 570).

In the summer of 1938, Miyoko came down with influenza, but she continued to overwork herself and remained sickly for a long time. In the latter half of 1939 beriberi affected her heart. [86]

POEMS 1940-47 [87]

In April 1941, eight months before Japan went to war against the United States, Miyoko spent a whole day viewing cherry blossoms in the ancient capital of Nara. [88] Poem 67 reflects this spring outing; about it Miyoko wrote:

> As I felt -- and yet almost with a tinge of resignation -- it would be my last spring to view the flowers to my heart's content, I (and my family) enjoyed ourselves in Nara Park. We did not yet have an actual experience of the B29 air raids, but my mind was constantly aware of a sort of black bird throwing shadows over the brilliant cherry blossoms. Even without this threat (of the war) their life would be short. And yet they overflowed in glory for one single moment of the day. I walked around on Nara Hill, cherishing the beauty, soon to be destroyed, as something eternal. [89]

While the dangers of war deepened Miyoko's awareness of inevitable destruction, the beauty of the blossoms intensified her appreciation of life. Her tanka recall a deep love for this particular flower -- *sakura kichigai* (cherry blossom craze) -- and her simultaneous admiration and apprehension concerning this delicate beauty.

In the afternoon, "as if the day's life declined before [she] knew," [90] the *sakura* on Nara Hill turned purplish in the weakening sunlight (poem 69). The symbolic association between day's end and the color purple was plain to her: life's brilliant variety of colors merges, at its end, into purple only. This color motif recurs in a more subtle and symbolic way in her later tanka: "Reflecting on the *"Tale of Genji "* (poems 121-130) and "The Color Violet," Miyoko's last published poems (240-246).

Her mother died on March 28, 1943; the poems about this loss are tender and present the mother as a person both defiant and helpless -- Miyoko's ironic understanding of life and death is emphasized in poem

73 when she speaks of "the shrouded sky" and the blooming cherries.

The Bankō Girls' School, founded by Miyoko's mother in 1919, had been run under these guidelines:

With sincerity and dedication.

Without ever asking for parents' donations.

With the total number of students not exceeding 120, with one class of 30 for each year of the four-year program.

With a faculty consisting of university professors and highly-qualified specialists in each subject.

During the war years, when Japanese schools were particularly reluctant to accept students from Korea and Taiwan, Miyoko's mother received them with kindness and impartiality. [91]

To keep this idealistic school operating, the fortunes of Miyoko's maternal grandparents had been exhausted and the Gotō estates mortgaged. After her mother's death, Miyoko rejected a favorable offer to purchase the school and take over the debt. Instead, she resolved to carry out her mother's wishes and take over as principal.

Although Miyoko was never an advocate of war, she frankly admitted her devotion to her country in wartime. That devotion was strengthened by her determination to preserve the Japanese language which could be threatened by foreign occupation. She had learned in Wales about the fate of Welsh people who were gradually losing their language under English rule. She also observed her Korean students, who were not allowed to speak in their own tongue. She feared a Japanese defeat would lead to a debasing and eventual loss of the Japanese language, and through it, of Japanese national identity.

The war ended with Japan's unconditional surrender on August 15, 1945. Suffering from a severe food shortage, the country struggled to rebuild itself out of its ruins; its society began changing rapidly. In October 1945, political prisoners were released and the Communist Party began making a vigorous comeback. In January 1946, the emperor formally renounced his "divinity" and in November a new constitution was promulgated. For the first time Japanese women had the right to vote and run for office; in December, thirty-nine women representatives were elected (see poem 77). A new educational system modeled on that of the United States was introduced in April of 1948, bringing co-education to high schools and universities.

Japan's resurrection from the ruins inspired Miyoko and she urged Hitomi and the students in Bankō Girls' School to pursue their development through higher education, now opened to women. Her chōka: "Prefatory Song to *Fire and Snow*," reveals the excitement Miyoko felt about this new future for Japanese women.

Her poetic life was remarkably productive. Numerous tanka vividly describe the chaotic society immediately after the war, characterizing it through juxtaposition: Japan's defeat, humiliation, hunger, hardships, filth and confusion were contrasted with carefree children under blue skies, brilliant flowers above the ruins, the sense of peace and companionship in a crowded train.

In an essay published in May of 1946, Miyoko voiced firm opposition against the general trend that regarded tanka as being anti-democratic simply because it is a traditional form of poetry. She argued that since the tanka innovations of the 1890s, tanka had been playing a significant role in the movement for women's liberation. Miyoko said: "Allow us to sing freely, and you will discover that tanka is the most democratic art form that can reflect directly people's and especially women's emotions" (HD, p. 240).

Miyoko's poetry during this post-war period reveals her inner struggle as well. Chilling winds (poems 84, 91 and 93) are frequent. During this period, an essay by Sakaguchi Ango (a writer well versed in Buddhist philosophy) supporting the view that the collapse of established values was a degeneration essential to the process of rebirth attracted many trendy followers. Miyoko's contempt for these people and their view of the confusion that Japan was experiencing is reflected in the last line of poem 92, "Fall, muddy yourself," which refers to a popular phrase that summed up Sakaguchi's philosophy of decadence.[92]

But Miyoko also celebrated the excitement of this period. Like many writers, she felt the surge of all the creativity that had been suppressed during war time. Although she found an affinity with the great literary traditions of Japan (especially with the *Tale of Genji*) her heart was "still not content" (poem 87). Something "sizzling inside" (Poem 93), drove her to seek out new expression.

In 1946, she was privately tutored in English poetry and she attended English language classes with Hitomi, who was preparing for her university entrance examination.

During the next four years, although Miyoko's relationship with Hitomi became very close again, the spiritual tensions between them increased. The ecstatic/apprehensive mother returns in poem 94, as if Miyoko's maternal instinct and her poetic intuition anticipate Hitomi's untimely death.

POEMS 1948-49 [93]

Hitomi graduated in March of 1948 from Tokyo Women's Higher Normal School. She then went on to specialize in English literature at Tokyo University, the school Miyoko had left twenty-two years earlier in order to devote herself to her daughter.

Miyoko, deciding it was time to resume her study of Japanese literature, passed a competitive examination for students who wished to attend lectures but not obtain a degree, and began studies at the same university as Hitomi.

Miyoko's younger daughter Izumi, then in her early teens, was often left alone at home. Though keenly aware of conflicts between her maternal responsibility and her desire for learning, Miyoko did not sacrifice herself this time. She believed that to be true to herself she must now devote herself to the utmost. She was convinced that her devotion to self-development would also serve as an inspiration to her daughters and her students.

In 1978, after her mother's death, Izumi wrote:

> She did not belong to the type of mother who welcomes the children returning from school in her *kappōgi* (cooking apron), who prepares a lunch box for a school excursion, or who dresses her children in homemade clothing. Rather, my mother went out to university lectures, leaving her young child alone till late at night, and when she was at home she wrote poems in the middle of night, as if possessed. With such a single-mindedness that it appeared almost foolish, she lived truthful to herself ... although she was never a 'good mother', she exemplified a life always earnest and sincere. [94]

The tanka Miyoko wrote about her daughters at this time were both sharp and tender. She observed the delicate physical changes occurring in Izumi, and the increasing psychological tensions between herself as mother/student and her older daughter Hitomi.

Again she occupies a fluctuating state of mind: "fire continues/ to burn in me, now blazing,/ now smoldering" (poem 105). She presents herself as a solitary, restless, and somewhat aloof poet who "live[s] in a corner,/ watching/ spotlights slowly shift/ as the world changes" (poem 100).

From time to time she also appears to merge herself into the universe. The quiet rhythm of the living universe seems to unite her with sparkling icicles in the valley (poem 111), with "tiny trampled grasses" (poem 109), and with a soft-thorned rose of early summer (poem 107).

Miyoko was reaching the peak of her creativity, experiencing more frequently those moments of the "demon's visit" when she felt her life "whittled away" as the poems came (poem 106). Such moments produced a number of the most memorable tanka of her life; among them are the deeply moving recollections of her parents' deaths (poems 97 and 103).

At the university, Miyoko joined a weekly seminar on the novel: *The Tale of Genji,* written by Lady Murasaki in the early part of the 11th century. Its fifty-four chapters depict the private and public lives of four generations of noblemen and women of the Heian period (mid-10th to early 11th centuries) and centers on the triumphant career, but principally on the loves, of the Shining Genji.

Miyoko had received her first formal training in this classic at the Institute of Japanese when she was sixteen. Eight years later, at Kokugakuin University, she studied the entire *Tale* in a year-long course.

The weekly seminar at Tokyo University was directed by the Genji scholar: Ikeda Kikan. Among the small group of student specialists was a young American scholar, Edward Seidensticker.

Miyoko's several valuable studies of *The Tale of Genji,* mirror the influence the novel had on her own compositions. Perhaps the most important of these was a lecture given in 1972 at the International Conference on Japanese Cultural Studies, sponsored by the Japan PEN Club. In it, she discussed the 42nd chapter of the book: "*Kumogakure*" (*Hidden Behind Clouds*), which contains no words and suggests Genji's death. Of this chapter, Miyoko says:

> If Lady Muraski should have decided to write anything in the chapter, she might very possibly have written only one character: *kū* (void). I feel that must be so. The *Tale* is composed to present the idea that "this world is in essence 'void'," and I think, therefore, nothing is written in this chapter ... (HD, p. 312).

In her studies Miyoko offered unique observations based on careful research and analyses. She showed particular interest in the last ten chapters of the *Tale*: "*Uji jūjō*," finding in them a tragedy of character that contrasts with the tragedy of fate in the proceeding chapters. Miyoko noticed that "when we reach the last ten chapters, we begin to see women act, for the first time in the whole tale, from their own independent will" (HD, p. 290).

Miyoko attended lectures on Buddhism in order to gain a deeper understanding of the book. In an essay entitled "*The One Book: The Tale of Genji*" (*Issatsu no hon, Genji monogatari*; published in the March 9, 1965 issue of the *Asahi*, a major daily paper), Miyoko wrote:

> If I were to choose the one book in all my life, I cannot help naming *The Tale of Genji*. Since fifteen or sixteen, I have never passed a year without reading it, each time finding it new and gaining a different appreciation (HD, p. 265).

In 1949 Miyoko composed a ten-tanka sequence entitled "Reflecting on the *Tale of Genji*." Her composition is perhaps the most important tribute to the classic ever written by a modern tanka poet.

Miyoko was remarkably original in her symbolic use of color images to sum up the rich, courtly life described in the *Tale*. The Heian nobles experience joy and sorrow, while the Buddhist world view casts its gray veil over the cherry blossoms and crimson leaves of their lives.

"Reflecting on the *Tale of Genji* " clearly demonstrates the depth of thought and mastery of expression that Miyoko's poetry had by now attained.

In 1951, Miyoko wrote an essay about the 45th chapter: "The Lady at the Bridge," in which she makes some observations about the novel that tie directly into her life.

In *The Tale*, the Eighth Prince (Genji's brother) lives a life devoted to Buddhist studies and refined practice of music. His wife dies after giving birth to their second daughter and the two girls are raised by their father, whose religious and musical pursuits are reflected on the young princesses' lives.

The 45th chapter (to which Miyoko's tanka also refers) depicts these two daughters as they play the lute and koto on a misty autumn night at their secluded villa on the Uji River. They are unexpectedly seen by Kaoru, a visitor who has come to see their father. Kaoru falls in love with the older sister, Ōigimi, but she turns him away and dies shortly after their father.

In her study of this chapter Miyoko, expressing a particular interest in Ōigimi, writes:

> The author of this tale must have aimed at presenting a new theme: platonic love. For the first time at least in the extant Japanese literature this theme was dealt with through the creation of Ōigimi, a woman of unique personality and upbringing (HD, p. 268).

Miyoko's meticulous analysis of the following passage from the chapter reveals her as an independent thinker. She challenges the generally accepted views as to which of the two princesses played which of the two instruments: the lute or the koto. This translation of *The Tale* by Edward Seidensticker describes the scene:

> The princesses were farther inside. Half hidden by a pillar, one had a lute before her and sat toying with the plectrum. Just then the moon burst forth in all its brilliance.
> "Well, now," she said. "This does quite as well as a fan for bringing out the moon." The upraised face was bright and lively.
> The other, leaning against an armrest, had a koto before her. "I have heard that you summon the sun with one of those objects, but you seem to have ideas of your own on how to use it." She was smiling, a melancholy, contemplative sort of smile. [95]

By referring to this and the scene as drawn in the 12th century Genji picture scrolls, Miyoko maintains that the princess with a koto is Ōigimi. She points out how the description of the girl matches those in earlier passages in the chapter: "The older girl was comely and of a gentle disposition, elegant in face and in manner, with a suggestion behind the elegance of hidden depths" (p. 776) and was "composed and meditative, quick to learn but with a tendency toward moodiness" (p. 777).

Miyoko's detailed analysis concludes that the characterization of Ōigimi carefully prepares for the development of a "Platonic love" between the pensive Kaoru and the "meditative" Ōigimi: Both characters are deeply interested in Buddhism; Kaoru is troubled by uncertainty about his birth; and Ōigimi, obedient to the words of her devout father, is determined to remain secluded from the world. When Ōigimi rejects Kaoru's sincere love, he tries to understand her:

> What, [Kaoru] asked himself, could have turned a young girl so resolutely away from the world? Was it that she had learned too well from her saintly father the lesson of the futility of things? But they were kindred spirits, he and she, and he could most certainly not accuse her of impertinent trifling (pp. 833-834).

Miyoko's next study on the Tale appeared two years later in March 1953 in the *Indogaku Bukkyōgaku* (*Studies on India and Studies on Buddhism*). Entitled "*Genji monogatari Uji jūjō ni egakareta ai to shi ni tsuite*" (*On Love and Death Described in the Ten Uji Chapters of The Tale of Genji*), the essay compares Ōigimi's love with that of other ladies in the Tale and comments on her death:

> Despite its femininity, gentleness and elegance, Ōigimi's rejection of a physical relationship with Kaoru shows something so deep that it never seems to be pulled out. This refusal, so strong and decisive, leads us to the problem of suicide: contemplating the inconstancy of human life, she reaches the denial of a carnal love between man and woman and consequently the annihilation of her own physicality (HD, p. 290).

Miyoko must certainly have associated Ōigimi's death with the death of her daughter, Hitomi.

In her article, "*The One Book: The Tale of Genji*" (1965) Miyoko says that her view of the Uji chapters changed around the time she lost her daughter (HD, p. 267) and both of these essays directly support this point. One was published as if it was meant to be Miyoko's requiem for Hitomi. The other appeared shortly before the day when Hitomi's ashes were finally buried (see poem 147).

POEMS 1950-59 [96]

On January 26, 1950, Kondō Yoshimi received a telegram from Miyoko which read simply: "Please come and see Hitomi." He rushed to the school building on the hill where the Gotōs lived:

> Hitomi was lying dead: it was a sudden death. As if alive, she was sleeping with her face covered with a gauze on a large bed in a room which was originally a classroom. Clinging to Hitomi, Miyoko cried until she was exhausted. With rouge touched on her face, Hitomi looked translucently beautiful.

> Like tatters
> you collapse in tears
> beside her;
> but see, I've witnessed
> death of such beauty.

Kondō ends his recollection:

> I have heard bits of stories about Hitomi: her anguish in the midst of the violent student movement at the university and the distress she felt about her unworthy love. Though only briefly, I came into the life of a person who quickly left us like a falling star.
> To the end of her life Miyoko never spoke of what "kyūshi" [sudden death] meant. [97]

In the original, his phrase: "unworthy love" was written "mazushii ren'ai" (poor love). This seems to imply that Hitomi, daughter of two well-known poets, loved someone who was socially unsuitable for her.

Miyoko, deeply shaken by this personal loss, closed her mother's school and was ill during most of 1951.

In July of 1953, Miyoko published: *Tanka Poems of a Mother*. The book, written to commemorate the third anniversary of her daughter's death, contained 427 tanka and two chōka about her children. Four years later, ninety-four tanka were added to the collection and *Tanka Poems of a Mother: New Enlarged Edition* was published. It received the Yomiuri Literary Prize in 1958.

Miyoko focused on her daughter in other works as well, resurrecting some quotes that commented on Hitomi's state of mind. In her essay: "About My Hitomi" (c. 1955), Miyoko recorded Hitomi's words:

> Mother, I was born and led you to create new tanka. My birth did something for you. If you are now in a slump, caught up with your mannerism, I will die for you. Then, you will produce fine poems again, and I will have done something for you once more (HD, p. 108).

These feelings, suggestive of irony, are echoed in Hitomi's diary: "I only live on out of duty to my parents. How hard it is" (HD, p. 108).

Contrary to the tone of these quotations, Hitomi did have much to her own credit. A classical, large-eyed beauty, she was also known as a bright, sensitive, and serious-minded young woman with potential all her own.

Hitomi, the product of a protective family was, however, very uncertain of herself, a trait shared by many young people of the post-war period, whose anxieties were enhanced by the conflicting values and ideologies of the times. Hitomi's tanka clearly show her ambivalence:

> He stands,
> carrying in his pocket
> a copy of *Central Organ*
> of the Communist Party.
> Something in me shrinks. [98]

and

> Campus billboards,
> left and right wing powers swirling;
> after so long
> I see them again, I recoil,
> a coward at heart.   (HD, p.106)

Once, Hitomi told her mother that she would prefer to stop thinking and throw herself into action, regardless of the consequences. She may have desired to participate in radical politics or have a deep personal commitment of her own, such as marriage, but Hitomi's nature seems to indicate the consequence she feared most was her parent's disapproval. She knew they would not have approved of either of these actions.

Miyoko knew that Hitomi had a temperament different from her own: she contrasted her own passionate "fire" with Hitomi's seemingly cool and critical "snow" (see "Postscript" to *Fire and Snow*, TGMZ, p. 192), but she prized her daughter's sharp, discerning mind. Miyoko treated her like an equal and even found a worthy rival in her. But Hitomi believed that the intensity she saw in her poet-mother could only belong to a genius and she felt incapable of living up to her mother's high expectations.

In his detailed commentary at the end of the *Definitive Tanka Collection of Gotō Miyoko* her husband writes:

The sensitive Hitomi was also quick to respond to other matters than her study. Her mother, who had once gone through that "One Stage" of her life [see **Poems 1924-30**], watched her daughter apprehensively. Miyoko's worries increased while they studied together. Hitomi's ideas and activities added suffering to her mother's anxiety, throwing darkening shadows between mother and daughter who competed with each other, sometimes even coming into conflicts (TGMZ, p. 597).

One day, Hitomi told Miyoko: "[I am] an ordinary, insignificant girl of little talent" (HD, p. 87), and to her closest friend she confessed: "It can never be easy to have a genius in the family" (*Risshun*, No. 32, p. 84).

So despite abundant talent and potential Hitomi regarded herself as a failure: a young woman unable to take action in a changing society, and the very ordinary daughter of a genius.

The chronology in Miyoko's *Definitive Tanka Collection* refers to Hitomi' death as *kyūshi* (sudden death). When this word is used without providing the cause of death it usually implies suicide.

In her essay on Hitomi's death, Miyoko states the cause as "acute bronchitis" (HD, p. 108). Despite this, her poetry, her essays on the ten Uji Chapters of the *Tale of Genji*, and Hitomi's own statements all indicate that there was something out of the ordinary about the death.

Miyoko's essays on *The Tale of Genji* set up a parallel between Hitomi and one of the heroines of the novel: Ōigimi, whose death Miyoko interprets as suicide. Both were distinguished for their delicate noble beauty; both died in their early twenties; neither had experienced a physical relationship. Miyoko writes: "Ever afraid that her mother would disapprove her fall, and anxious not to hurt her, Hitomi died a virgin" (HD, p. 107). [99]

Critics and commentators of Miyoko's poetry tacitly agree that Hitomi killed herself, possibly for ideological reasons. Still, they avoid using the term *jisatsu* (suicide) because they lacked concrete evidence to support their views.

The poems in the following tanka sequence refer to one of Miyoko's friends whose son killed himself about the same time as Miyoko lost Hitomi:

She whispered,
"My son, who had taken
his life,
courted me in my dream."
My friend, his mother, don't go mad.

In her dream
my friend married
her dead son.
Did he enter once more
his mother's womb?

A season of
bereavement for me and for her;
in my maddening sorrow
my friend consoled me, but
she, too, has now lost her son   (TGMZ, p. 242).

In Miyoko's tanka collections these three poems are not placed as a sequence independent from the other tanka. Thus, when the reader fails to note the sequential context of the three, the lack of gender indicator in Japanese could mislead them to this reading:

Her friend whispered that
my daughter who had taken her life
courted him in his dream.
Friend and mother we must not go mad.

In this version, "Her friend" would refer to Hitomi's boyfriend. Interpreting the poem this way a Japanese critic took it as the key to the mystery of Hitomi's death: he deduced she had killed herself.

This interpretation, however, is not consistent with the other two tanka in the sequence. Consistency would require the second poem to read:

In his dream
her friend married
my dead daughter.
Did he enter once more
his mother's womb?

The ambiguity of gender in the original poem makes it possible to use either gender in the last two lines of this tanka. Either way, the translation still does not substantiate the critic's interpretation.

The translation initially given for the first tanka in the sequence corresponds to Mr. Gotō's explanation about who committed suicide. He claims that the poem refers to the tragedy that Miyoko's friend experienced, that she wrote these poems because she was deeply moved by her friend's grief.[100] In addition, they explore a subject that was new to tanka: the Oedipus complex as revealed in her friend's dream.

Although no one has been able to substantiate the suspicion, it does appear that Miyoko was hinting at a parallel between the two deaths. The phrase, "the dead child that took its life" appears only once in the *Definitive Tanka Collection of Gotō Miyoko*. This suggests the poet may have counted on the controversy that would be generated by a single appearance of this phrase. Ironically, by keeping the cause of her daughter's death a mystery Miyoko created a legend of the suffering mother; she was determined to atone for the death of her daughter by turning her suffering into poetry.

After her daughter's death the public aspect of Miyoko's life included two important appointments to which she devoted herself until her death.

She became, in 1955, one of the three editors for the tanka column of the *Asahi* daily newspaper. For twenty-two years, Miyoko dedicated herself to selecting the best from the thousands of tanka submitted by people of all ages and from all walks of life.

Her commitment reflected her belief that the tradition of tanka would live as long as ordinary individuals could find a true voice of the heart to feed the form. This idea not only circles back to proletarian influences, it also shows how deeply Miyoko valued amateur poets. She also selected for a tanka group of members of the National Federation of Textile Workers. [101]

In 1959, Miyoko was appointed tanka instructor to Miss Shōda Michiko, now Crown Princess of Japan.

Although Miyoko was immediately captivated by the lady's beauty, from the first lesson, on January 19, 1959, she was a strict teacher. As the future Crown Princess had never before written tanka, Miyoko instructed her:

> However painful and shameful you might find it, you should compose tanka as if you are baring your soul before God. You must forget your status, and must not try to write skillful tanka that would pass as decent. You have to sing of even what is ugly in you as if you make a confession to God. For my part, just as a priest will never reveal a confession and just as a

doctor will never show his patient's chart, I will never let anybody see your poems (HD, p. 323).

Miyoko advised her student to practice writing one tanka a day for one hundred days. She also asked her to memorize those classical tanka included in the lesson.

From January to March 1959, in nine weekly sessions each lasting two hours, Miyoko was impressed by the dedication of Miss Shōda, who despite the mounting pressures of the forthcoming royal wedding made remarkable progress. Miyoko even suggested that Miss Shōda select one hundred of her best tanka to present to the Crown Prince as her wedding gift.

Miyoko continued to serve her student after she became Crown Princess and her admiration for the woman increased as years went by. In her essay: "Crown Princess" (1973) she proudly referred to two of the princess' published tanka:

This child is mine,
but like a treasure entrusted
into my arms,
he fills me with awe
as I embrace him.

How vivid
his crimson lips;
my baby
sucks, the thick white milk
overflowing.

(Written in 1960; HD, p. 329)

POEMS 1960-69 [102]

Miyoko's two daughters were not only different in character and appearance they were influenced by different social environments.

Hitomi graduated from a prestigious municipal high school in Osaka. Half of her college career occurred during a time when war and ideology imposed rigid disciplines on Japan, demanding obedience and conformity to militaristic thinking.

Izumi, eleven years younger, was educated under the new school system introduced after the war, under a new ideology that promoted liberal and democratic thought in both students and faculty.

Hitomi, small, delicate and introspective, was much like her scholarly father; Izumi was outgoing and shared her mother's feminine attractiveness.

Hitomi, alive, had been a sharp critic of Miyoko's poetry; after her death and while Miyoko was ill, Izumi prepared the manuscript for her mother's fifth tanka collection. Later, when Miyoko was hospitalized for viral pneumonia, Izumi handled all her "daily affairs" (poem 162).

In her chōka, "Even If I Were Crushed Down" (1946), Miyoko wrote about an incident on a crowded train when Izumi was nine years old. Izumi told to her mother not to worry: "Even if I were crushed down, I am all right, because I'll grow tall again" (TGMZ, p. 159). These words not only comforted her mother, they made the tension-packed crowd relax into laughter. They foreshadow Izumi's development into a woman of independent mind, capable of overcoming difficulties in order to pursue her own way. On July 29, 1962, Izumi was seriously hurt in a car accident; hospitalized for two months she got engaged to Kamo Bunji, an official of the Ministry of Finance. They married on December 8, 1962, at St. Ignatius Chapel where Izumi had been baptized nine years earlier.

In Japan it is felt that marriage is brought about through *en*, a mystical bond between the couple's families through which the partners are destined to meet. Yet Miyoko's poems (167-173) show her in a complex emotional state as her daughter is about to leave her to get married. Her uncertainty seems to begin with concerns about aging. In poem 164, she pictures Narayama, the hill where old people are taken to die in the novel *Narayama bushi kō* (*The Song of Oak Mountain*). [103] She is defiant, (poems 165, 166 and 173), and she fears more dull contentment (poem 172). As the tanka turn to the subject of marriage, she voices resentment (poem 168), but tries to restrain herself from interfering in Izumi's life. In "Having Lost My Child" (*Ko wo ushinau*), an essay that was written about six months after Hitomi's death, Miyoko speaks her concerns to her dead daughter:

> After all, does your mother continue to live on only in order to raise and pull up your sister Izumi to the brilliance you reached? But even your mother appears to become gradually accustomed to lead a life always with one step held back, as she fears that your sister, too, might die young, if she were brought up as you had been (HD, p. 88).

On returning from a trip to Kyūshū (one of the four major islands of Japan, facing the Eastern China Sea on the west; see poem 177), Miyoko became ill and was hospitalized for cholecystitis. Convalescing at a resort on the Pacific coast, Hayama, she portrays sorrows of motherhood by commenting on sea-turtles laying eggs (poem 178).

In July 1963 her son-in-law was appointed Chief Taxation Officer in Akashi, near Osaka. Izumi accompanied him, but soon returned to Tokyo to give birth to a baby girl, Yukari, which means "relation" or "bond." Izumi left the baby with her parents so she could rejoin her husband and Miyoko found a new sense of life through the grandchild. She also felt a strong connection between this baby and her dead daughter (poems 184 and 185).

During this same year, Miyoko published the *Gotō Miyoko zenkashū* (*Collected Tanka Poems of Gotō Miyoko*), the most important publication of her career. It contains 2283 tanka and 12 chōka, written between 1921 and 1963, most of which had previously appeared in five separate collections. She edited this collection during the summer while the baby lived in an incubator.

After a year in Akashi, Izumi's husband was transferred back to Tokyo, and the Gotōs reluctantly returned Yukari to her parents, a separation that only increased Miyoko's concern about a possibly desolate old age (poem 187).

This feeling intensified when in 1967 Yukari's father was assigned to the Japanese Embassy in Rome. As departure drew near, Miyoko's attachment to her granddaughter grew particularly intense. In poem 188 she expresses her loss, stating she is "not able to turn into / a demon of attachment / or even a peaceful old woman."

In this poem, the word "attachment" translates *aishū*, which is a Buddhist term consisting of two characters: *ai* (love) and *shū* (to cling to, or to be attached to). *Ai* is one of the "twelve causations" that keeps living beings caught in the cycle of birth and death and *aishū* implies the clinging type of love that Buddhism sees as a cause of suffering:

> Both fuel and air must be present for a fire to blaze up; so the fire of the passions is born from a combination of a sense-object with imagination .... It is the presence or the absence of imagination which determines whether attachment takes place or not. Supreme exertions should therefore be made to bring about a restraint of the senses; for unguarded senses lead to suffering and continued becomings ....
>
> And the mind which is dependent on the body involves us in such ills as grief, discontent, anger, fear, etc. Whenever there is a psycho-physical organism, suffering is bound to take place; but for him who is liberated from it there can be no

suffering, either now, or in the past, or the future. (*Buddhist Scriptures*, tr. by Edward Conze [The Penguin Classics], pp. 104 and 113).

This view of suffering is clearly reflected in Japanese literature, and especially in the Uji Chapters of *Tale of Genji* and the medieval Nō plays where focal interest is in the intensity and complexity of suffering, not in it's extinction. The characters, deranged by emotions such as remorse, anger, or jealousy, often turn into demons (*oni*). In her poem, Miyoko is struggling with a desire to possess her grandchild and seems to regret her inability to transform into one of these demons.

Unsettled by her emotions, Miyoko flew to Rome to spend Christmas with her granddaughter. Anticipating their reunion (poem 189) she longed to hold Yukari in her arms. She felt a kind of reincarnation had taken place, that Hitomi had returned to live in Yukari and was visiting foreign lands again, just as she had done when the Gotōs travelled in Europe (poem 190).

The student riots at Tokyo University in 1968 reminded Miyoko of the radical movements that occurred just after the war and the profound impact that they had on her daughter. Even though eighteen years had passed, the riots found Miyoko still struggling to understand Hitomi's death (poems 192 and 193).

Miyoko had to wait four years for her granddaughter to return from Europe (poem 195). Finally back in June 1971, she was supposed to come to live with her grandparents, but this never happened. In fact, Miyoko was not allowed to see her granddaughter as often as she wished, which only intensified her yearning.

In poem 199, one of seven in a group titled "*Aishū*" and also in poem 200, Miyoko speaks about their relationship as if they were in love. She describes her love for her granddaughter as "*koi naranu koi*," which literally translated means "love which is not love" (TGMZ, p. 382).

In Japanese, both *koi* and *ai* mean love, but *ai* (like it's English counterpart) is applicable to any kind of affection; *koi* is more suggestive of "yearning" and usually implies love between a man and a woman.

Kawabata Yasunari comments on these feelings in his introduction to one of Miyoko's collections:

> Miyoko seldom writes about extraordinary events outside her family life and only has a small number of descriptive nature tanka. Her poems are personal, indeed, but never dull, ordinary, or filled with the commonplace expressions frequently found in tanka about a private daily life centered on one's family and immediate relatives.
>
> To deal with one's familial experiences is in the very nature of tanka itself, yet Miyoko's poetry leads us to surprise, and we marvel at her uniqueness. Some outstanding examples are the tanka expressing her feelings for her granddaughter. They read like a lover's poems rather than a grandmother's. They present not fond thoughts of, but love-longing for a grandchild ["*magoomoi no uta*" and "*magokoi no uta*," respectively]. They are pure and intense, and their freshness is a wonder.

A youthful passion blazes throughout her poetry. Her tanka, expressions of powerful emotion with a touch of innocence and naivete, do not belong to the elegant and traditional tanka. Yet, far from being simple and refined, or monotonous, they strain to say so much within the formal brevity of tanka.

In other words Miyoko indicates she has that little-girl quality which is occasionally found in outstanding women artists. It is this quality that purifies and elevates the passionate and intense nature of her poetry. While going beyond the simple naivete of a little girl, both by preserving and nourishing the purity and originality of her art, this quality creates problems in the artist's daily life. This very quality [of going beyond] causes Miyoko to look into the depths of the demonic world, and to become aware of the loneliness of life; it also leads her to be driven by ceaseless love-attachment and to communicate with the spirit of the dead: here Miyoko's poetry contains something frightful (*Risshun*, No. 213 [May 1968], pp. 1-2; TGMZ, pp. 603-604). [105]

There are two intertwined reasons for Miyoko's separation from her granddaughter.

First there was the unusual bonding that echoed her involvement with Hitomi. In C. G. Jung's article: "Psychological Aspects of the Mother Archetype" he points to a pathological and possibly destructive aspect of this type of mother/daughter relationship: when the older woman throws her dark shadow over the child and arrests its normal development. Jung cites the example of Demeter, who kept her beautiful daughter Persephone in Sicily; when she was carried away by Hades, god of death, Demeter in grief wandered all over the world looking for the kidnapped child. [106]

About one year after Hitomi's death Miyoko wrote a tanka that mirrored this condition:

Blinded
by my clinging attachment,
I chase
after my daughter in Hades --
I know she wouldn't like it.

(TGMZ, p. 236)

Secondly, Izumi was having a difficult time in her marriage. It soon ended in divorce and when in 1974 she married a young sculptor, Yukari was placed in her father's care. He also remarried, accepted a three-year appointment in Geneva, and took Yukari with him.

Miyoko was tormented by having failed to recognize the problems and prevent the divorce. Condemning her inadequacies, she calls herself a "stupendous fool" (poem 204) and a bold tone of self-abandonment enters her poetry, as if her pent-up anguish can no longer be held back (poems 197, 198 and 202).

This new phase of Miyoko's poetic development is symbolized by "*tarumi*": the water from melting ice running freely over rocks in a stream. The term is used in the title of her seventh tanka collection. In her postscript to the collection Miyoko links her suppressed feelings to this kind of melting ice (see TGMZ, pp. 406-7).

The day before Miyoko wrote the postscript she quoted her tanka teacher, Sasaki Nobutsuna, in a letter to Tamaki Tōru, who later included the quote in his article, "Requiem for Miyoko":

In composing tanka, never falsify your heart's truth, but give it your honest expression. However, when you publish your tanka in newspapers, magazines, you must not publish those

tanka which, you think, according to socially-accepted good
sense, may bring harm to others or may disturb the peace of
your family.

Miyoko confessed in her letter that she had become increasingly aware
that her creativity had been suppressed by her teacher's advice. She was
beginning to feel that she might go mad; her heart was filled with
things she wanted to express yet felt could not say. She asked Tamaki:
"... should I be heedless of troubles I might cause to others -- even to
close relatives -- and turn into a demon of tanka?" This question,
Tamaki observed, showed she already was a "demon of tanka." [107]

Intensified by her granddaughter's second absence of four years
(1974-77), Miyoko's longing spilled into her poetry and Yukari
frequently appears in her thoughts, dreams, and visions (poems 206,
210, 217).

When the Gotō's went to Europe for their golden wedding
anniversary Miyoko looked forward to seeing Yukari; they visited the
house in Geneva but were not allowed to see the child.

Miyoko's disappointment was intense. Upon her return to Japan she
developed the ulcers and the liver disease that resulted in her death
within less than three years.

During these final years, having transformed all her pent-up
emotions into physical symptoms, Miyoko's mind and soul began to
approach a state of resignation and peace. In this process of change her
granddaughter still occupied her thoughts (poems 207 and 217). Her
physical pain was both the effect and constant reminder of the tragic
estrangement from her only grandchild, ironically arousing her sense of
still being alive (poem 214).

A calm detachment of spirit, however, came to pervade her tanka,
which place her in harmony with simple things: birds, calves, potatoes
and fruit, all of which helped, both physically and spiritually, to bring

peace back to her life. Images of her granddaughter and recollections of her visit to her son-in-law's studio in Rome (poem 212) reflect the gentle chiaroscuro that marked the final phase of her life and creative work.

POEMS 1977-78 [108]

When Yukari returned from Europe in July of 1977 she visited her grandmother at the Ōtsuka Cancer Research Institute Hospital in Tokyo. She was shocked to see how emaciated Miyoko had become. Yukari couldn't make herself approach her grandmother and Miyoko was so overcome that all she could do was gaze at her grandchild. [109] Unfortunately, this was to be their last meeting. Yukari went to see her grandmother twice more, but Miyoko was in a coma during both visits.

Despite her illness, Miyoko was extraordinarily creative during her last year; she composed 142 tanka and even gave occasional lectures. The best work of this period is represented by three tanka sequences: "The Storm of Blossoms," "Lingering Blossoms Dance in Frenzy," and her last published tanka, "The Color Violet" -- all linked to cherry blossoms (see p. 124).

Miyoko seems to sum up her whole life through the image of cherry blossoms. In the first two sequences, flowers she saw in the past seem to mingle with those she now sees in her yard. [110] She watches the frenzied dance of the lingering flowers (poem 232) and yearns to soar to the sky with the storming blossoms (poem 224).

On February 6, 1978, Miyoko was brought home from the hospital in a wheel-chair. Gravely ill, she was stirred by faint signs of *risshun* (the arrival of spring). [111] The soft violet color of spring dusk enveloped her and turned into utter blackness. In their darkness she attained a serene awareness of being alive and that night she began to compose the sequence: "The Color Violet." [112]

The seven tanka were completed during the following night and published in the March 1978 issue of *Tanka Study*. They were the last poems to appear during her lifetime and serve as her final testimony to the tradition of *mono no aware* or pathos: the typical Japanese response to beauty tinged with sadness.

In his postscript to *The Flower Clock* (1979), a posthumously-published collection of Miyoko's essays, her husband wrote:

Last year (1978) the cherries bloomed later than usual.

Miyoko died at dawn on April 15th and in death she came home for the first time in fifty-four days. That morning we found what Miyoko described as 'lingering blossoms' on the slope of our yard. When daylight broke after the vigil, the 'storming blossoms' still veiled our sight (HD, p. 331).

Notes

Notes

1 For Kawabata's words see *Teihon Gotō Miyoko zenkashū* (*The Definitive Tanka Collection of Gotō Miyoko*), ed. Gotō Shigeru (Tanka Shimbun Sha, 1983), p. 617. Hereafter this book will be referred to as TGMZ.

The place of Japanese publications is Tokyo, unless otherwise indicated. The Japanese titles are translated on their first reference and given in English on subsequent appearances in the text. The Japanese titles are used in bibliographical references for those who might wish to consult the original.

Japanese names are presented surname first. For example, Kawabata Yasunari, Gotō Miyoko, and Gotō Shigeru (Miyoko's husband). Her first name, however, is used when referring to the poet.

2 The *Kokinshū* (or *Kokinwakashū*), the first imperial anthology compiled around 902, has been traditionally esteemed as a collection of exemplary tanka.

3 *Nyonin tanka* (*Women's Tanka*), No. 30 (December 1956), pp. 551-65.

4 "*Kemono no nioi*" (*The Smell of an Animal*), *Tanka Kenkyū* (*Tanka Study*), January 1951, p.28.

5 Gotō Miyoko, *Hanadokei* (*The Flower Clock*), ed. Gotō Shigeru (Shiratama Shobō, 1979), p. 91. *Hanadokei* will be abbreviated as HD.

6 Tamaki Tōru, "Miyoko chinkon" (Requiem for Miyoko), *Tanka*, July 1978, pp. 363-364.

7 *Shishōsetsu* is a confessional novel based on the author's personal experiences and usually narrated in the first person singular. It is often characterized by narrowness in scope and by triviality, which have invited harsh criticism. But not all *shishōsetsu* deserve such criticism; some are fine pieces of literary work.

8 Gotō Miyoko, "*Naze tanka wo eranda ka*" (Why Did I Choose Tanka?), *Tanka kenkyū*, May 1957, p. 133.

9 "*Watakushi no tanka shō*," (Selections from *My Tanka*), *Risshun* (*The Arrival of Spring*), No. 400 (January 1985), pp. 61-72; HD, pp. 250-251. See also *Watakishi no tanka* (*My Tanka*; Shibata Shoten, 1957), pp. 13-27.

   Risshun is the organ of Risshun Tanka Society established in 1938 by Gotō Shigeru and Miyoko. This issue commemorates the 400th publication of the journal.

10 Tamaki Tōru, *Tanka jissaku no heya* (*The Room In Which Tanka Is Created*; Tanka Shimbun Sha, 1983), p. 115.

11 Ueda Miyoji, "Sengo no shūka (59)" (Post-War Masterpiece Tanka: 59), *Tanka kenkyū*, September 1982, p. 138.

   For English translation of *Kojiki* see *Kojiki*, tr. Donald L. Philippi (Princeton University Press, 1969), pp. 55-63.

12 *Risshun*, No. 400, p. 76. See also *Watakushi no tanka*, p. 33.

13 "Tanka to no deai" (Encounter with Tanka: a Symposium), *Nyonin tanka*, No. 43 (March 1960), p. 10.

14 *Tanka jissaku no heya*, p. 79.

15 "Tanka to no deai," *Nyonin tanka*, No. 43 (March 1960), p. 10.

16 Eric Amann, "Form in Haiku," *Haiku*, Vol. 2, No. 2 (1968), p. 2. *Haiku* a pioneering haiku journal, was founded and edited in 1967 by Amann and lasted until 1970. It was succeeded by *Cicada* in 1977 also under his editorship.

17 *Ibid.*

18 "You" in the second line refers to Ishigure Shigeru, now Miyoko's fiance. Miyoko's parents had a summer house on the Tone River; the third longest in Japan, it flows through the Kantō Plain into the Pacific Ocean. Miyoko crossed the river to go to the summer house.

19 The poem refers to the young couple's honeymoon at Karuno.

   In tanka practice notes can occasionally be placed at the beginning of one or more poems; sometimes such a note may appear at the end instead.

20 See quote about holding Hitomi in **1924-30: Commentary**, p. 112.

21 Hanare Hill is a landmark hill in Karuizawa, a fashionable summer resort on the plateau at the foot of a live volcano, Mt. Asama, about 150 km. north of Tokyo.

22 Salted pickling paste, *nukamiso*, made of salted rice bran, is commonly used for pickling vegetables. On winter mornings housewives do not like to put their hands, often roughened, into the cold salty paste.

23 Shoulder tucks can be taken down when children grow and sleeves become too short.

24 The poem was occasioned when Miyoko and Shigeru founded their tanka society, *Risshun* (The Arrival of Spring). "That day" refers to the day when in 1915 Miyoko became a tanka student of Sasaki Nobutsuna (see **1898-1923: Commentary**, p. 128).

25 For explanation of *ashura* see **1931-39: Commentary**, p. 120

26 See **1931-39: Commentary** [p. 121] for explanation of Kishimojin.

27 The chronology in the *Definitive Tanka Collection of Gotō Miyoko* informs us that the poet had a type of influenza in the summer of 1938 and after that her overwork left her in a long sickly condition. She also suffered in the latter half of 1939 from beriberi.

28 "My daughter" refers to Hitomi, now thirteen years old.

29 See **1940-47: Commentary** [p. 122] and note 88 concerning Nara Hill.

30 With her older daughter Miyoko washed and dressed her mother's corpse. See also Poem 102.

31 This poem refers to Japan's unconditional surrender on August 15, 1945.

32 This tanka echoes a well-known chinese poem, "A Spring View" written by one of the greatest Tang poets, Tu Fu (712-770). His first two lines read:

The nation shattered, hills and streams remain.
A city in spring, grass and trees deep.

(Burton Watson, *Chinese Lyricism*, [Columbia University Press, 1971], p. 162).

33 *Fire and Snow* is Miyoko's third tanka collection published in 1952 and contains 315 tanka and 6 chōka composed in the years 1946-1948.

34 Although Miyoko was never an advocate for nationalist war efforts, she frankly admitted her blind devotion to her country at war.

She explained her war-time devotion by her determination to preserve the language of the Japanese race which might have been threatened by foreign occupation. (See HD, p. 172 and **1940-47: Commentary**, p. 123).

35 *The Tale of Genji* was written by a court lady, Murasaki Shikibu, in the early 11th century. It is regarded as the world's first great novel. See **1948-49: Commentary**, p. 127.

Man'yō poems are in the *Man'yōshū* (*Ten Thousand Leaves Collection*), the earliest extant collection of Japanese poetry compiled in the latter half of the 8th century.

36 The last line of this poem alludes to *Darakuron* (*On Degeneration*) by Sakaguchi Ango (1906-1955). Sakaguchi's essay appeared in the April and May issues of the *Shinchō*, an influential literary journal. In June 1947 it was published in a book of the same title.

37 The Musashi Plain is part of the Kantō Plain, the largest in Japan. The Gotō's house is in this northwestern area of Tokyo metropolis.

38 After his autopsy the brain of Miyoko's father was preserved at the Medical School of Tokyo University where he was professor emeritus.

39 This phrase is derived from the English expression.

40 "The picture scrolls" in the poem signify the Genji scrolls of the 12th century attributed to Fujiwara no Takayoshi (dates unknown). Miyoko refers to them in her essay *"Genji monogatri Uji jūjō shikan: 'Hashihime' no kaishaku ni tsuite"* (My Personal View on the Ten Chapters of Uji of *The Tale of Genji*: Problems of Interpreting the Chapter "The Lady at the Bridge"). This study, first published in the February 1951 issue of *Kokugo to kokubungaku* (Japanese Language and Literature), is now collected in *The Flower Clock* (see HD, pp. 267-284). Miyoko presumably saw the scrolls by the time she composed the ten tanka on the tale.

Until the early 14th century pigment made of plumbous white was used for the base coat. After rough sketches were drawn in black ink on the white base, colors were painted thick. Then black-ink lines were drawn again. Facial features were added in a manner known as *hikime kagibana* (each eye drawn in a long slightly curved line and the nose in a hook-like line a little below the wide space between the eyes). Painting was completed with a touch of vermilion for the lips.

41 See discussion on "Lady at the Bridge" in **1948-49: Commentary**.

42 The hanging bamboo screens were usually used to protect the women of the Heian aristocracy from being seen by visitors. The poem refers to the screens both metaphorically and physically.

43 The poem seems to allude to the death of Genji, the Shining Prince, hero of the Tale. Its 42nd chapter is called "Hidden Behind Clouds" and has no words written in it, suggesting Genji's death. Also see **1948-49: Commentary**, p. 128.

44 The type of cremation practiced in Japan leaves a mixture of ash and bones; after the cremation the bones are picked out by the nearest kin.

45 *Koto* is a zither-like instrument with thirteen strings under which moveable bridges are set at specific distances for tuning.

46 This poem refers to Miyoko's friend, also a tanka poet. Also see **1950-59: Commentary**, pp. 137-139.

47 It is unusual to keep at home an urn containing ashes for three years: normally its burial takes place within a couple of months after cremation; until then the urn can be placed on the altar in the temple to which the family belongs.

48 In 1952 the United States carried out the first test of an hydrogen bomb. It was followed a year later by Russia's success in making a similar bomb. In March 1954, Japanese fishermen suffered serious radiation sickness caused by "ashes of death" from the American hydrogen bomb test in the Bikini area.

   The exact date of this poem's composition is not known, but its location in Miyoko's *Definitive Tanka Collection*, which follows the chronological order, suggests that the poem was written around 1953, instead of 1954, in which year the ill effects of the Bikini tests were much discussed in Japan with anger and anxiety. The United States and the Soviet Union competing in their hydrogen tests, the poet might have foreseen the panic the Japanese were to experience early in 1954.

49 The baptism was given at the St. Ignatius Chapel of Sophia University in Tokyo.

50 For this annual event thousands of tanka are submitted from all over Japan and even from overseas countries, such as the United States and Canada, and about fifteen are selected. The topic for composition is announced the year before. *Hayasi* (Woods) was the topic for 1954.

51 *Kunugi* is a kind of oak.

52 Poems 158 and 159 deal with Miss Shōda Michiko, now the Crown Princess of Japan.

53 In the summer of 1959 the Gotōs had a summer cottage built in Karuizawa where the hill is located.

54 In the Japanese society the succession of a family line is still taken into consideration in deciding on a marriage when a family has no son but a daughter.

Miyoko's parents took their son-in-law, Shigeru, into the Gotō family. Miyoko regarded Izumi, now the Gotō's only child after Hitomi's death, as their heiress, and might even have found a predestined link between herself and her daughter. This situation might partially explain Miyoko's strong desire to take into the Gotō family Izumi's child, again a daughter, who is Miyoko's only grandchild.

55 In August 1960 Miyoko was hospitalized for viral pneumonia.

56 Narayama is the hill to which old people are taken to die in a novel, *Narayama bushi kō* (1956; "*The Song of Oak Mountain*" tr. by Donald Keene) by Fukazawa Shichirō (1914-). Its film version won the *Palme d'Or* at the 1983 Cannes International Film Festival.

57 In Japan a marriage is traditionally considered not to be accidental, but brought about through a certain bond (*en*), by which not only the couple is destined to meet, but also their families are somehow linked generations before their actual marriage.

58 "My teacher" here refers to Sasaki Nobutsuna under whom Miyoko began in 1915 her formal tanka study.

59 This poem and the succeeding one refer to Miyoko's involvement in the proletarian tanka group.

60 Hayama, a resort on the Pacific coast, is about 50 km. south of Tokyo.

Once, during their stay at Hayama, Mr. Gotō recalls, they were shown sea-turtle eggs by local fishermen who believed that while laying their eggs the turtles actually shed tears.

On her return from the trip to Kyushu (one of the four major islands of Japan, facing the Eastern China Sea on the west) Miyoko was hospitalized for cholecystitis.

61 See **1960-69: Commentary**, pp. 143-144 about "*aishū*"

62 This poem refers to Hitomi's funeral in 1950.

63 In the mid-1960's, as in the West, many universities in Japan suffered from violent student riots.

64 *Uwamizuzakura* is a variety of cherry. In May its small white blossoms bloom in clusters. It bears bean-sized berries. The tree stands in the center of the Gotōs' Karuizawa estate with a stone monument on which this poem is inscribed together with her husband's tanka:

> In the sky
> autumn winds circle
> the volcano --
> a torrent of sounds
> over the earth.
>
> (Written in 1964; *Hiraku* [1979], p. 92)

65 See **1970-76: Commentary**, p. 145 concerning "*koi naranu koi.*"

66 See note 105.

67 "It" in the second line refers to Izumi's relationship with the young sculptor whom she married later.

68 The poem deals with Miyoko's failed attempt to see her granddaughter in Geneva.

69 The poem refers to the studio of the sculptor son-in-law in Rome which the poet and her husband visited on their trip to Europe in 1975.

70 "The Storm of Blossoms," containing 51 tanka, first appeared in the May 1977 issue of the *Tanka*. Eleven out of the fifty-one poems deal with the storming cherry blossoms Miyoko saw in the spring

of that year.

71 The four tanka on lingering blossoms that dance in frenzy are taken from the seven-poem sequence on this topic. They were among the thirty tanka published in the June 1977 issue of the *Tanka kenkyū* (*Tanka Study*).

72 Samurai retainers who served domanial lords (*daimyō*) were rewarded for loyalty with grants of land rights and serfs. But when these vassals became more like administrative officials than land-based warriors, their annual stipends were paid in rice or its money equivalent. These salaries were hereditary, and yet they could be increased, decreased, or confiscated at the lord's pleasure.

   After *daimyō* domains were abolished in 1871, the new government paid pensions to the former samurai as compensation for the loss of their hereditary income. But this privileged arrangement did not last long due to the heavy financial burden on the government; payments were converted into interest-earning bonds, and other measures were taken to help the ex-samurai to enter new careers (e.g. government subsidies and sponsorships).

73 Quoted by Watanabe Sumiko in her *Nogami Yaeko kenkyū* (*A Study of Nogami Yaeoko*; Yagi Shoten, 1969), p. 56.

   In May 1972 Yaeko began the serialization of her fifteen-chapter novel, *Mori* (*The Woods*), which deals with the pioneering women educated at Meiji Girls' School. Only the latter half of its last chapter was left unfinished when she died on March 30, 1985, thirty-seven days before her 100th birthday.

74 The Rescript, promulgated in 1890, defined the fundamental aims of education for the new Japan which was undergoing a vigorous transformation into a Westernized nation, while retaining its emperor system. Since both the political system and traditional family principles were the basis of the nation's educational

objectives, the edict promotes Confucian virtues, especially loyalty and filial piety. At the same time it encouraged new knowledge and the edification of a responsible citizen for the advancement of the new modern state.

The government distributed copies of the Rescript to schools, where students were required to memorize it and principals were instructed to read it to the students on special ceremonial occasions such as national holidays. This practice served to propagate Japan's nationalistic policies, but it was discontinued by the Occupation after the end of World War II.

75 *Kunugi* is a kind of oak.

"The Iwamotos" refers to the family of Iwamoto Yoshiharu the head of Meiji Girls' School; Shinko-chan is Miyoko's younger sister, her only sibling; Yutani was a teacher of Japanese at the school.

Yaeko's poem was published in the Gotō Miyoko memorial issue of *Risshun* ([*The Arrival of Spring*], No. 328 [July, 1978], p. 50).

76 *Shidome* is a thorny shrub about 30 cm. tall and its flowers bloom in spring.

77 Railway grass is also called *Meijisō* (Meiji grass), coming from its original home, North America, early in the Meiji era.

78 Two chōka (long poems) and 244 tanka (and four given in the notes) are selected for this translation from the *Teihon Gotō Miyoko zenkashū* (*The Definitive Tanka Collection of Gotō Miyoko*, 1983). One exception is poem 145 which is found in *Shinshū haha no kashū* (Tanka Poems of a Mother: New Enlarged Edition [1957], p. 157). In the poem section of this text, to the right of each translated poem, you will find a consecutive poem number followed by the

poem publication date (which usually corresponds with the year of composition).

79 Poems in this section come from *The Warm Current* (1936).

80 See Kawada's preface to *Danryū*, (TGMZ, p. 37).

81 For Shino Hiroshi's article: "Shinkō tanka undō no kōzō" (The Structure of the Movement of the Newly Rising Tanka Poets' Group), see *Tanka*, February 1983, p. 142.

82 See *Ishigure Shigeru tanka shu* (*Tanka Collection of Ishigure [Gotō] Shigeru*; Nihonhyōronsha, 1929), "Postscript," p. 4.

Two examples from Shigeru's collection clearly show his influence on Miyoko's poems during this period:

> The crowd breaks up:
> stiff and hollow
> white buildings soar above them.

> Playing with my daughter
> I see a flash of Marx's face: he, too,
> crawled on the floor with his child.
> (*Ishigure Shigeru kashū*, pp. 4 and 192).

83 See Shino's article above, p. 146.

84 This collection of proletarian tanka was edited by the Tanka Zen'ei Sha (Tanka Avant-garde Society) and published by Marukusu Shobō (Marxist Publisher) in September, 1930. For Miyoko's poems see *Provetaria tanka shū*, pp. 69-71.

85 See *Watakishi no tanka*, pp. 64-65; *Risshun*, No. 400 (January 1985), p. 95.

86 This kind of beriberi, which often caused heart failure, was common at the time among Japanese who lived on refined white rice.

87 Poems in this section come from *On the Hill* and *Fire and Snow* (1952).

88 An expansive park located in the eastern part of the city of Nara, an ancient capital, about 30 km. south of Kyoto.

89 *Watakushi no tanka*, p. 678; *Risshun*, No. 400 (January 1985), p. 96.

90 *Ibid.*

91 *Risshun*, No. 338 [January 1984], pp. 9-10.

92 See "Darakuron" (On Degeneration) by Sakaguchi Ango (1906-1955) in the April and May 1946 issues of the *Shinchō*, an influential literary journal.

93 Poems in this section come from *Fire and Snow* and *The Wind* (1950).

94 *Risshun*, No. 328 (July 1978), p. 174.

95 E. Seidensticker tr. *The Tale of Genji*, (Alfred A. Knopf, 1977), Vol. 2, p. 785; subsequent quotations from the *Tale* come from this translation.

96 Poems in this section come from *The Wind* and *I Am Alive* (1961).

97 From the 11th installment of the serialization "*Utai koshi kata*" (As I Sang Along This Passage of Tanka; Iwanami Shoten, 1986), pp. 86-87) where Kondō Yoshimi (1913-) records the night of Hitomi's death.

    Director of the Society for Modern Tanka Poets, Kondō Yoshimi has also been serving as a selector for the *Asahi Tanka Column* since its establishment in 1955.

98 Though the political party's name is not included in the original, the terms, "*tō chūō kikanshi*," suggests to the Japanese the Communist party.

99 As Buddhism played an important role in Ōigimi's view of life, we find in Miyoko's tanka these words: "Near her death / I hear, my daughter asked / about religion. / Today again I trace /

her heart's path." (TGMZ, p. 225; composed in 1950 soon after Hitomi's death).

100 This explanation was given to me by Mr. Gotō at an interview.

101 Miyoko served as poem selector for the tanka group of the National Federation of Textile Workers and supported this federation as well as Democratic Socialist Party of Japan until her death. See *Risshun*, No. 409 (October 1985), p. 2.

102 Poems in this section come from *I Am Alive*, *Time Difference* (1968) and *Falling Water* (1975).

103 *Narayama bushi kō* (1956; "The Song of Oak Mountain" tr. Donald Keene) by Fukazawa Shichirō (1914-).

104 The poems in this section come from *Falling Water* and *The Storm of Blossoms* (1978).

105 Kawabata Yasunari (1899-1972), a novelist, won the Nobel Prize for Literature in 1968; killed himself on April 16, 1972; Miyoko refers to his death in poem 201.

106 "Psychological Aspects of the Mother Archetype", *The Collected Works of C. G. Jung*, tr. R. F. C. Hull, [Bollingen Series XX; New York: Pantheon Books Inc., 1959], IX, Part 1, pp. 75-110.

107 See "Requiem for Miyoko", (Miyoko chinkon) *Tanka* (July 1978), pp. 363-64.

108 Poems in this section come from *The Storm of Blossoms*.

109 In our conversation in the summer of 1984 Yukari, the poet's granddaughter, gave me this account of that pathetic meeting.

110 Miyoko had planted about twenty mountain cherries along the winding paths on the slope of the Gotōs' garden in Tokyo.

111 According to the lunar calendar the arrival of spring usually falls around February 4th. The term, *risshun*, is also the name of the tanka group led by Miyoko and her husband.

112 It is also significant that Miyoko uses both "violet" (*sumire iro*) and "purple" (*murasaki*) alternatively. Purple was the poet's favorite color; she often chose it for her gala clothes. The color carries a strong association with *The Tale of Genji*; we recall that Miyoko's ten tanka sequence on the *Tale* ends with the lines: "purple sorrow / lingers until absorbed / into the void" (see poem 130).

Bibliographical Note*

In her lifetime Gotō Miyoko published seven books of tanka: 1. *Danryū* [*The Warm Current*] (Sanseidō, 1936); 2. *Oka no ue* [*On the Hill*] (Osaka: Kobun Sha, 1948); 3. *Honoho to yuki* [*Fire and Snow*] (Risshun Tanka Kai, 1952; this volume, completed in 1948, is regarded as Miyoko's third tanka collection, because its poems belong to a period preceding that of the next book, which appeared earlier); 4. *Kaze* [*The Wind*] (Nyonin Tanka Kai, 1950); 5. *Inochi arikeri* [*I Am Alive*] (Kadokawa Shoten, 1961); 6. *Jisa* [*Time Difference*] (Shiratama Shobō, 1968); 7. *Tarumi* [*Falling Water*] (Shiratama Shobō, 1975). The eighth collection, *Hana tagitsu* [*The Storm of Blossoms*], was edited by her husband, Gotō Shigeru, and published by Tanka Shimbun Sha in 1978. The first five collections were included in *Gotō Miyoko zenkashū* [*Collected Tanka Poems of Gotō Miyoko*] (Tanka kenkyū Sha, 1963).

Miyoko also published several books of selected tanka, among which the most important is *Shinshū haha no kashū* [*Tanka Poems of a Mother: New Enlarged Edition*] (Shiratama Shobō, 1957), which received the 1958 Yomiuri Literary Prize; the first edition, *Haha no kashū* (*Tanka Poems of a Mother*), was published by Risshun Tanka Kai (Risshun Tanka Society) in 1953. A fine selection of 221 tanka and three chōka (long poems) from the eight collections is given in the 328th issue of *Risshun*, journal of Risshun Tanka Society, published in July 1978 (three months after her death) in memory of the poet.

Miyoko also wrote three books dealing with tanka composition: *Fujin no tame no tanka no tsukuri kata* [*Women's Guide for Composing Tanka*] (Osaka: Semba Shoten, 1942); *Tanka no tsukuri kata* [*How to Write Tanka*] (Shufu No Tomo Sha, 1952) with one thousand examples written by women, corrected and commented on by the author; and *Watakushi no tanka* [*My Tanka*] (Shibata Shoten, 1957). Fortunately a substantial portion of the now out-of-print *My Tanka* is reprinted in the commemorative 400th issue of *Risshun* which was published in

---

* Unless otherwise indicated the place of publication is Tokyo.

January, 1985. There are many other essays and critical writings, one posthumous collection of her prose works is *Hanadokei* [*Flower Clock*, ed. Gotō Shigeru] (Shiratama Shobō, 1979).

Teihon Gotō Miyoko zenkashū (*Definitive Tanka Collection of Gotō Miyoko*) edited by her husband, who contributed an illuminating, extensive commentary on Miyoko's life and poetry, was published by Tanka Shimbun Sha in 1983. Miyoko's previous eight volumes of tanka are brought together in this definitive edition; it contains 3918 tanka and 13 chōka, and a detailed chronology that is the source of the one given here.

A number of commentaries and criticisms of Miyoko's poetry can be found in various tanka periodicals such as *Tanka* and *Tanka kenkyū* (*Tanka Study*), as well as in the commentaries, prefaces, and postscripts written by poets, novelists, and critics for her collections, but no single critical book devoted to her work has yet appeared. Most important of the periodical pieces is Tamaki Tōru's "*Miyoko chinkon*" [*Requiem for Miyoko*] (*Tanka*, July 1978, pp. 362-371).

**The Poems
In Japanese**

The Poems in Japanese

1. ありし日は神になげきし思^{おもひ}なりわが歌はただ祈^{いのり}に同じ

2. 君をおきてふたたび越ゆる大利根や岸のまこもの黄ばみわたれる

3. いねがてにひとり撫づればはしきよし君が息吹^{いぶき}にふれし黒髪

4. 天地^{あめつち}は月の光となりにけりふといぶかしむ二人あることを

5. おごそかに吾^{われ}によりくる一歩み吾はも終^{つひ}に母ならましか

6. 胎動のおほにしづけきあしたかな吾子の思ひもやすけかるらし

7. ほのぼのと明くる光に目を合はせ今は親ぞとわれらを思ふ

8. 身にそへておかれし吾子^{わこ}に見入りつつ涙とまらずなりにけるかな

9. 自分と顔を見あはせてゐるやうな不思議な気もち子とゑみかはす

10. あぶないものばかり持ちたがる子の手から次々にものをとり上げて
    ふつと寂し

11. いひたいことにつき当つて未だ知らない言葉吾子はせつなく母の目を見る

12. はしたない叱言にあつて立ちすくむ子の眼いちはやく母をうつしつ

13. はなれ山の絵といつて子の描くを見れば空につきぬけたいくつもの道

14. あの道が天まで突き出て見えるのかと子を抱いて仰げば山の姿がちがふ

15. せい一杯両手をのばして抱かれようとする子は日に向かふ草花のやうに

16. だまりこくつてゐることが唯一の反逆であつた私の過去

17. ごみ箱のやうな暗闇に疲れ切つた心だこの梅の花は白すぎる

18. 新鮮な空気と日光のなかにみすぼらしい自分の姿よ書斎から出て来た

19. 疲れを空に吸ひとらせようとする口笛昼休の職工は野を歩きまはる

20. 子を遊ばせてゐる私の方をじろりと見て午後の仕事に帰つてゆく
    職工の一人

21. 思ひ切つてぬかみその冷たい朝だ今日も又行路病者が死ぬのだろう

22. 何といふ腑甲斐ない今日の私 一本の指の皹^{あかぎれ}が心までかじかませるのか

23. 夫が帰らなければ地球がまはらない様に思つてゐる自分は未だ
    やくざな女だ

24.　目の色を変へて特価品の山をかきまはしてゐるおかみさん達に
　　　　突き飛ばされる

25.　夜業廃止記念会並んで座つた女工の後姿に未だ深ぶかとした
　　　　肩上げを見る

26.　黙つて話をきいてはゐるがあの凝固つた頭の中に銃丸の様に飛込んで
　　　やりたいのだ

27.　煙草のけむりと一緒に消えた彼らの結論だ吸ひがらは給仕が
　　　　片づけてゐる

28.　自分の子には決してさせる日がないと安心して危険な作業の前を
　　　　通り過ぎるのか

29.　追つて出た子の洟をかんでやる間もなしにやつれた母は工場へいそぐ

30.　やつとしつかり吸ひついた赤ん坊の口から母の乳房をもぎはなす
　　　　午後の汽笛

31.　右左から子にまつはられて米とぐ母のあらはな胸にぢかにさす西日

32.　足どりが鈍いのは明日の世の担ひ手の子供を抱いてゐるからだ女達を
　　　　おいて行くな

33.　お互同志の空腹に響きあふものをじつと抱へて黙つてゐるのか
　　　　お弁当のない子達

34.　空腹をこらへる事に馴れてゆくこの子達の強さを畏いとおもふ

35.　夜明近づくけはしい寒さだ明日の光にいきづく迄風邪引くな子供達よ

36.　口紅著るくさまよふ街の娼婦たちともしげにわが子を振りかへる

37.　母性の相ふとあらはれてよりどなし紅粉の底の街娼の顔に

38.　みなり貧しき子供ばかりが出で遊ぶペイヴメントに日は疾くかげれる

39.　しろじろと屋根みち光りけさは霜　別れ住まむとは誰がいひ出でし

40.　首飾の玉ちぎりて棄つる如く二人住む日の数を減らせり

41.　痛がゆきわが胸に似ていらだたしく濃霧の空に赤らむ月なり

42.　モンスウン　来らんとすと　ブリッヂの　報伝はれば　畏れつつも　した待つ
　　　心あれ　吾子連るる　この旅なれば　手まはりの　物片づけて　目も合はず　い
　　　ねし一夜は　事もなし　明くる光を　よろこぶと　デッキに上り　見さくれば　エ

ンヂンの音たえまなく　人間の意志を　調べつつ　マストは歩む　空のみち
艫にくだくる　波一すぢ　しろじろとしてはろかなり　天地の　天を高く　地
を低く　思ひしこころ　陸にゐて　思ひ馴れゐし　こころは遠く　無限広大の
宇宙の　ただ中に　かそかにも　われはあれ　上もなく　下もなく　前後左右も
なし　印度洋上　きはみなく　荒天をふくみて　もだす一時　すべなくはたと
思ひふれし　生の身の　わが生命　このいのち　すぎむとならば　今も死ね　屍と
なるとも　はしきやし　同じ地球の　上なりと　おほらにたのむ　こころは生れ
ぬ　かくてやうやく　時過ぐれば　風はたはたと　天幕を煽り　胸さきかけて　突
き上ぐる如　船は大揺りに　揺り出でつ　見るがうちに　空の彼方に　飛びあがり
斜ひに曲る　水平線　次ぐ瞬間は　舷の　下いく丈に　沈みゆく　すはこそ　嵐は
来れと馳せ降りて　船室の窓　かたく閉ぢ　ベットによりつつ　固唾のむ　真ひ
るまの　光を僅か　径尺の　丸窓に得て　ひそみ居るに　忽ち暗む　天地の底　沈
む船かと　おもほゆる　その時の間に　光り散り　くだけ流るる　波がしら　滝つ瀬
なして　窓を過ぎゆく　一波こゆれば　ただに明るみ　再びはらむ　潮のもと　吸
はるる如く　低まるわが船　かくする中に　耐へかねて　ますらを君も　ころぶ
せば　心しめられ　なよる子を　胸にかくみて　なぐさもる　言葉はあれど　たよ
りなき　身に近近と　のしかかり　そびゆる波は　黒黒と　空をふたぎて　ほとほ
とに　窓のガラスも　打破らむと　くだけかかれば　ははそばと　思へるわれも
こらへかねむとす

43.　しぶくしづく窓一面に天地は潮けぶりしてただよふ吾生命
44.　親子三人いのち一つに凝る時しとどろき鳴りて海は揺り動く
45.　誰かにさはつてゐたいと死の床にまだたしかなりし父はのらしき
46.　夏光る病院の庭にざくろの花赤かりしかなつひに父は見まさず
47.　甕の中に生き残りゐるこほろぎは父が手ふれしめをとこほろぎ
48.　この日頃うるほひ深む吾子の瞳にをとめうごきてあやふきものを
49.　身を突き上げ深夜をしきる胎動にわれをゆだねてこころ足らへり
50.　ひそやかに母により来て胎内のはらからにと吾子のものいふらしも

51.　みなぎらふこの春のひかり胎内の吾子も浴みよと息づきてゐる

52.　月見草茎だち高くなりにけり産月の身に触れてかなしく

53.　上の子の児生ひいまだ目に濃きにこの子の顔が重なりて映る

54.　魂あへぎ一生の道を定めたりしその日も空は松に蒼かりき

55.　子を抱き妄念熄む時はあらず餓鬼道修羅道身に近しと思ふ

56.　自が子らを養ふと人の子を屠りし鬼子母神のこころ時にわが持つ

57.　くもりしるき鏡ぬぐはむ鋭心もなくなりて久しけふも微熱あり

58.　耳とほり今朝ほれぼれとききてゐぬ二人の吾子がそれぞれの声音

59.　わがしらぬ健やかさもちて育つ娘はわがをとめの日の日記よみて笑ふ

60.　ある日より魂わかれなむ母と娘の道ひそひそと見えくる如し

61.　物思ふかとしたおそれうしろまもりゐし母にあかるく娘は振向けり

62.　わが手の小指一本につかまりて三歳子の歩みしなひ重るも

63.　子の影法師地に濃くなりぬ線たどりて描きつつかなし両方の耳

64.　女身の道さからひかねてをとめづく娘はまみうるみ時にすなほなり

65.　ひそやかに花ひらきゆくこの吾娘の身内のものにおもひ至りつ

66.　身はもえて歩み停むるきりぎしにこの荒海の潮しぶきあがる

67.　黒き怪鳥影さす春とおもひをり咲きあふれさくら匂ふまひるま

68.　金色の蜂とまりゐて物の音も花にくぐもる昼山ざくら

69.　陽の光たまゆら変る動きありむらさき帯びきて花はしづむも

70.　こころかげ花に映りて明暗のほのかなるかといく度見なほす

71.　よくぞ勝ちたまひしとおもひ今は小さく幼子の如き母の背さする

72.　まかせたまふうつそみの骸燈に映えておほふすべなくいます母かも

73.　くもり日の空にあやふくまぎれむとさくらは咲けり母なき国に

74.　屈辱は苦く冷たく初の味鮮らしくさへ身に沁みわたる

75.　国敗れて残る山河のかくばかり花いつくしき春にあひにけり

76.　つなぎあふ手にしるき血のこのぬくみ落花ぼやけて子らとたたずむ

77.　忍従の果ての一言声はなく女ら去れり投票箱の前を

78. 野草摘む女童(めわらは)のむれえびがにとる童児幾人外(いくたりと)は青き光

79. 焼あとの土ほこりみち限なしじんともえつく陽は真上なり

80. 起きぬけの 頭ふりつつ けふもまた 痛む首すぢ もろ肩ゆ 腕ひぢかけて 松の木の 皮か張れると かさかさに 血の気うすれぬ よろこびて 国に死なむと きほひたる ありし日のこと 次々に めくられてゆく 真相に てらし出づれば 胸しらけ 面ほてりきて 内深き この疲れなり 朝鏡 身の衰へを うつすとき 心はもえて われとわが 瞳(め)に見入りつつ 女わが 身内(みぬち)の炎 消えぬまに いまひと度を 起きなほり このいのちもて 二千年の 史(ふみ)に未だ見ぬ この時の 女の歌を うたひあげむ 詠(よ)みひらかむと すべもなく 気息(いき)はずみくる うしろより 髪かがやきて さしのぞく 二十(はたち)の娘 いつしかも をとめ育ちて 人生(ひとのよ)の ことあげつらふ この子らが ゆき着かむ日の この国の 女の道の 遠白く 光りて見ゆるを 夢とはおもはじ

81. 窓あかるき木々の黄葉(もみち)は日に透(す)けりをんな子親子四つの眼見合はす

82. 子に生くる甘さはすてぬ子もわれも蒼空遠くはてなき道あり

83. 氷かたくどざせる奥に棲む(すむを)魚はまみ青からむ透(すき)とほり見ゆ

84. 身を揉めばかわきし音たつすべなさに小笹もわれも風に吹かれをり

85. 押込みし車内すきまなし揺られつつ耐へあひつつある静けさを感ず

86. 眼に沁みて花はうつくし泥濘(ぬかるみ)に一ひら散りて見るみる汚(よご)れぬ

87. 源氏よみ万葉(よ)誦みてかよひあふ心に足らずわれのさまよふ

88. 混濁の暗さに浮びしづかにもさくらは匂ふ春ほの白み

89. 夜となるを忘れたる如き夕空の蒼久しきに雲さへもなし

90. 時として草の香きつくよみがへる子供の日噛みし草の茎の香

91. 月と吾を一つにこめて吹き渡るま夜なかの風は冷気したたる

92. 髪ふりて空を仰ぎぬ堕ちよ汚れよとちまたに満てる声さげすまむ

93. 武蔵野のおそ秋風は吹きさます底たぎちま昼ほてるわが身を

94. 光あつまる吾子が姿を秋風の吹きさらふかと見れば危ふく

95. 親と子の血のぬくみあまり身に濃きにてれあひて子も眼をそらすらし

96.　引きむしる如く吾子よりはなれ来てもの学ばむと今日もきほへる

97.　夜半さめて近かぢか恋ほし東大医学部のアルコールに漬ける
　　　　　　わが父の頭脳

98.　力いつぱい生ききりて吾の枯るるときおのづから子に移るものあらむ

99.　こだはらず己が道ゆけと子にいひつつわが意識下にあるもの畏る

100.　おもむろに脚光移る世の動き片隅に生きてまなこ見はれり

101.　燃えやすき枯枝に似る身一つを吹きめくる風いつまで冬なる

102.　われと娘と深夜よそひしなきがらの母の重みは今も手にあり

103.　なきがらの母の乳首を花の如あかかりきと見しは錯覚なりけむ

104.　われ一人やしなひましし母の乳焼かるる日まで仄（ほの）に赤かりき

105.　降り消ゆる雪に競（きほ）ひて燃えさかりもえいぶりつつ絶えぬ炎あり

106.　ありありとけづらるる生命おぼえあり歌生るる時をしたに畏るる

107.　とげさへも柔かなりし初夏のばら心に持ちて木枯にゐる

108.　ごみつぼき枯芝にまじる若草はよごれ早き子の髪の匂ひす

109.　ひしがるる小草を見ればむねほとび滲（し）み出づるものに吾も救はれぬ

101.　縄とびの波に乗らむとたゆたひし稚なき日（いとけ）より吾は臆（おく）しぬ

111.　溶けなむとして日にひかる垂氷（たるひ）あまたしづくするとき谷は生きたり

112.　原人の祖（おや）の血ありて大地ぬくむ春にかばかり溶けゆくこころか

113.　半面のかがやき思ひわがねむるこの半球は春の闇なり

114.　をとめづかむとしてたゆたへる童女吾子きのふとけふの変貌うごく

115.　子よ母も育たねばならずある時のわが空白に耐へて遊べよ

116.　一人ゐて身をめぐるものの線の美に気づきしか子ははにかみてゐり

117.　恋人の如く責めあひて母と子はつひにしづかに手つないで寝る

118.　子には子の計算ありていふ言葉とび立てばみな小鬼のかたちす

119.　いためあふこころ意識にのぼる時われも子もいてふの梢見上げし

120.　飛び立たむ身じろきしるき子のけはひ　撓（しな）ひ失せし腕に抱きとめがたし

121.　胡粉剝落（ごふんはくらく）しげき絵巻にかいかがみ墨がきの線の勁（つよ）きにふれぬ

122.　川霧の流れの中に楽のねのくぐもりけむは昨日の夢かも

123.　銀さびて月澄む色は世を古りぬふりがたく生きてのこる言の葉

124.　五衣かさねて深き色めより心のひだの匂ひこぼるる

125.　言はまほしきこといはざりし息深くこもりてくしき女の業なり

126.　紅に黒を重ねて見る如き花花のいろ巻まきのこころ

127.　にび色の時の流れに花もみぢ散りぼひ浮かぶ相とらへぬ

128.　底澄みて女のひとみ見すゑたり香くゆり彩うごく几帳の中をも

129.　底つよく簾の外見出す女の眼おさふれどたをやげどまぎれぬ鋭さ

130.　つひのすがた光うすれて紫の愁ひはながく空に吸はるる

131.　この向きにて初におかれしみどり児の日もかくのごと子は物言はざりし

132.　物言はぬ子をかき抱きにはかにも時の流れの遠のくきこゆ

133.　汝が霊とも鬼ともなりて生きつがむ吾に苛責の鞭ゆるめざれ

134.　松うごく風見てあればまさやかにそこに生けりと吾子を思へり

135.　わが胎にはぐくみし日の組織などこの骨片には残らざるべし

136.　白百合の花びら蒼み昏れゆけば拾ひ残しし骨ある如し

137.　ひとみいい子でせうとふといひし時　いい子とほめてやればよかりし

138.　空が美しいだけでも生きてゐられると子に言ひし日ありき子の在りし日に

139.　空の美しいのも子が生きてゐてこそとかの日言はざりしゆゑ子に
　　　　死なれしか

140.　琴柱たて風にまかせてゐたりけり冬枯の丘にひびく空鳴り

141.　死にたゆる同胞のなかにわれひとりうごめき生きて水を欲る夢

142.　目さむればいのちありけり露ふふむ朝山ざくら額にふれゐて

143.　いつまでも埋まらぬ空所ひとところ亡き子の席なほ風吹きぬけて

144.　母の胎ふかくふたたび入りにしか友が夢見し亡き子との結婚

145.　天地に亡き子みなぎり降りにふる春雪の痛み処に沁む

146.　亡き子来て袖ひるがへしこぐとおもふ月白き夜の庭のブランコ

147.　むせぶばかりの若さにあへぎ生きゐたる吾子の骨かと頬にあてつつ

148. 憎みあふ心空に爆ぜ灰ふれば山の水さへ掬ひがたき夏
149. ひざまづきめぐみを享くる子のうしろ吾は聖母の像にまむかふ
150. 夫も子もいねて久しき夜半の灯に何にたかぶり窓おし開く
151. 身にふれてくぬぎ若枝はしなふなりをかの林の道ほそくして
152. けものめく匂ひをたつる時ありて娘が長き髪梳くはなやまし
153. のどもとに突き上ぐるものありてうたふ新聞投稿歌に女名多し
154. 口ごもりふつふつたぎるものにあへぐ女の歌にあひてたじろく
155. どもりつつ訴ふるもの切なきに稚き字のあと暫く見入る
156. 鉛筆のさきとがるときおちつきぬわが内の要らぬもの捨て去らむ
157. 花とけもの一つに棲めるをとめ子はひる深くねむり眠りつつ育つ
158. 朝露に翅しめる蝶たゆたひて舞ひのぼらむとす空の蒼みに
159. まをとめの想ひゆたけき歌百首身に添へもちて嫁きますきみは
160. 娘が騎りし桔梗が丘ははるかにて瑠璃色の空うつすとおもふ
161. 娘の顔もかさなりて映る朝かがみ女嗣ぐべき家の窓にて
162. 世のこと皆いづみにまかせて歌よめと入院のわれに子がくれし文
163. いかづちは陰にひびきてとよもせり死ねよとおもふ人ひとりもつ
164. 雪とづるなら山の道みえてゐぬこの夜ひそかに何おもふ子は
165. わがために生きむとおもふ第一日陽は炎えさかる立体に見ゆ
166. 灰いろのわが髪ひとすぢ炎え七彩なせば若さ蘇りぬ
167. つひにあひえし一人のひとと子があればわれは卵のからの心地す
168. われをはなれ嫁く子うべなひ足らひつつ憎みに似たるおもひもきざす
169. 嫁く日近みもの縫ひ更かす娘のけはひ襖ごしにききてわが目冴えゐる
170. 前の世に何をちぎれることありてこのひとり娘をゆだねむとする
171. きれいなもの新しいもの好きなものかき集め子は日々はこび出す
172. 限りなく足らひ安らふこのこころ危ふしかくて老いむとするか
173. 老いせじとあらがふこころあるときは子ら遠ざけてわれの爪とぐ
174. 「ひろく深くおのがじしに」の師の教へ仰ぎつつ来し半世紀のみち

175.　内乱をおこせの指令手にうけてくびすかへせしは三十のとき

176.　暴力をにくむこころ身に突きとほりそのとき熱きわが血に聴けり

177　東海の潮に浮かぶ日本列島弓なりに花咲きつがむとす

178.　女身かなし海亀は砂に大粒の涙おとして卵生むとふ

179.　子をうみしおぼえある身にひびき来て吾子のみごもりいや深むころ

180.　幽界とつな引きあへる日夜にてこの児いつの日むねに抱かむ

181.　生まれ来てはじめてあへる春の雪このみどり児の眼と光りあふ

182.　乳汁かれて胸にあふるるもの切なしこの子いだけば身内うづきて

183.　忘れゐしどこかの部分動き出してよる昼やまず子育てはげむ

184.　逝きし子の魂よみがへるこの子かと真夜おもふとき長き息づき

185.　逝きし子をこの子の伯母と言にいひて何かそぐはぬ寂しさを感ず

186.　加速度にいのち過ぎゆくわが日日とすれちがひゆく児の生ならむ

187.　かぎりなく愛しきものと別れ棲み老いすさまじくきく風の音

188.　愛執の鬼ともならず静かなる老にも入らず日日の孫恋ひ

189.　さびしければ洋梨をむきて食べてをり洋梨の肌はをさな児に似る

190.　生きて再び訪ひ得ずなりし国国に娘のみたまかけれと入れし異国貨

191.　こふる子につひにあひ得むローマの空の明けの茜よ一生わすれじ

192.　かく叫び罵りたかりし日もあらむとり乱しかねて死にし娘の顔

193.　ふうせんを両手に天路ゆきたしと思ひつめし後娘のいひしかも

194.　うはみずざくらの朱実につどふ山の鳥朝食夕食の時さだまれり

195.　たんぽぽの絮毛吹き吹き児とゆきし春のひかりをまた浴みむかも

196.　人踏みし月面まなうらに鮮らけしさあれどかくも若く細き月

197.　憤ることありし日は夜ふけてチャンバラ劇にこころ放てる

198.　逃げ走る悪漢の画像見つつふと逃げおほせよとねがふ心あり

199.　愛するといふは傷つくことなりと七十にして身にしみて知る

200.　あひたしと言にはいはず言はさむとする孫八つ恋のすべ知る

201.　たよらずにゆけと宣らすかわが歌にたまはりし言葉今も生けるに

202. 己が身を実験台とし詠まむ歌、恍惚のかなたもプラスとなさばや

203. 松高きくもり日今日は亡き母のみたまかそかにものいふらしも

204. 気づかざりし悔いの八千度われといふ大迂疎祖母声あげて泣く

205. 流行歌の常はおぞまし恋の言葉孫うたへばわが涙腺たへず

206. 幻の児にたうべよとむく梨の汁したたりて寒夜ただ一人

207. 孫に見せむと植ゑし苗木の山ざくらことしの花は空をおほへり

208. 父の日に二輪目の百合ひらきたり見よと父よぶ声ふときこゆ

209. 風になびき腰にも散りし洗ひ髪父と見る花庭に光りき

210. 透明の大き箱に入りて物思ふ孫と夢見てけさうつつなし

211. 空ゆ来しおもひただ一つひと目見むとねがひしにあはず帰らむとする

212. 椅子ひとつ片よせられて床にころがるくらき塊みな顔もたむとす

213. 母われに負はせし傷の深きほど浮き上り娘は今きらめけり

214. 痛み止むひとときの空白耐へがたし生きゐることのあかし失ふ

215. 山の鳥と食分けあひて木の実草の根身をやしなへば和む朝夕

216. 土にまろぶジャガ芋互ひにうなづきあふ大きはもだし小さきは声して

217. 牛の乳牛の仔に分けてもらふ日々乳つくりやりし日の孫顕つ

218. かなし孫海わたり来む年とおもふをとめづく身に潮の香まとひて

219. 花たぎつ　幾十年見来し春なれば花びら重なりてまじりあふ翳

220. むらさきににじむ葩ありたまゆらを茜さすあり夕花吹雪

221. 散りまじりたぎつ花びら空にあり風に段なし時になだれつ

222. 花の奥に花あり更に奥に顕つまなかひの花まぼろしの花

223. いのちありてあひ得し春は病み惚けさらぼひて花の呼吸に負けゐつ

224. 痛きところあれば身は地にくぐまれど花たぎつ日は空も翔けたし

225. 花吹雪は地に散るものと思ひゐし天霧らひ空も人もおほへる

226. ことしの花いろすこし淡しいく春の匂ひうしろに濃く顕たしめて

227. 目の奥に花あればふぶく花あらしにうつつより濃く散りかひこむる

228. 花の中にうごく影ありたぎつ瀬なしくづるるときのうつくしさ痛く

229. 見て来たる暗き世おもへば嘘の如く花咲き揃ひ月も満ちたる

230. ことしの花　目にしみ心にしみ入りて胃の腑痛めば更に胃にしむ

231. いづくよりともなく散りくる花ありて夢のこる日々胃の痛み刺す

232. 花乱舞ときありて誘ふ風待ちて吹雪するさま酷薄なり

233. 散る見れば未だ多かりし梢の花枝にかへらむとくるめき舞ひ立つ

234. わが胃壁のただれ見せられし春たけて真白き花花梨・つつじ・鈴蘭

235. オーロラの青き炎ともえ尽きむ北まはり来む孫と眼あはば

236. 花の香も風にのりてはまひ来むにわがおもふ子のけはひだにせぬ

237. 雲間より見つめてありしかなし子のふと横向くと見てさめにけり

238. 限りなく愛しきものと逢ひ見つつなほやみがたき愛執は何

239. 血を分けし身にもまかせぬ愛し子を恋ひわびて病むおほ母かわれ

240. すみれ色に昏れしづみゆく大地に春ふくむ匂ひそことなくあり

241. 深みゆくいろ何いろと考へてすみれのいろと思ひあたれる

242. すみれ色濃きもうすきもひと色に菫のいろと昏れなづみゆく

243. いのちありてまた見る空も大つちもすみれの色にたゆたひて暮る

244. 深まれば黒くさへ見ゆる闇のいろもと紫と知りてなづさふ

245. すつぽりとすみれの色に包まれて闇に息づけどわれ生きてあり

246. 生きるといふ大きなること紫のすみれの色と今一つなり

Poems Quoted in Commentary and Notes

Gotō Miyoko (五島　美代子)

自殺せし亡き子夢に来て求婚せしとささやく友よ母よ狂ふな

われにもありし狂期の時期をなぐさめし友もわれも子をうしなひし季節

死に近く宗教のことも訊ねしといふ子のこころあと今日もたどれる

冥路まで追ひすがりゆく母われの妄執を子はいとへるならむ

Gotō Shigeru (五島 茂)

くづれゆく群集を

左右から壓^{あっ}して

かたく うつろな ビルデングの白さ

よつんばひになつて子供と遊ぶマルクスの顔が ふと見ゆ

　子とあそびつつ

火の山の虚空に充てる秋風のあふるるごとく土に音立つ

Gotō Hitomi (五島 ひとみ)

党中央機関誌をポケットにして立つ人に矢張たじろぐもの我にあり

左右勢力うづまくアーケードにひさしぶりにきて後しざりする

　わが生活態度

Crown Princess Michiko (美智子東宮妃)

あづかれる宝にも似てあるときは吾子^{わこ}ながらかひな畏^{おそ}れつつ抱^{いだ}く

ふふむ乳のま白きにごり溢れいづ子のくれなゐの唇生きて

Kondō Yoshimi (近藤 芳美)

ぼろの如君はかたへに泣き伏せどかく美しき死をば吾が見き

Index
of First Lines

Reiko Tsukimura, Professor of Japanese Literature at the University of Toronto, was born in Tokyo and studied at Japan Women's University. She received a Ph.D. in Comparative Literature from Indiana University and has held academic positions at the University of British Columbia, Harvard University, and University of Minnesota.

The Lake, her translation of one of Kawabata Yasunari's most unusual novels, was published by Kodansha International in 1974. Her many articles in English and in Japanese reflect a major interest in the dynamic interplay between Japanese and Western culture and between tradition and modernity. This is well demonstrated in the present work, a thoroughly researched and perceptive interpretation of the life and poetry of Gotō Miyoko.